Consciousness is Awareness

An Exercise in Self-Discovery

Dr Shannon Panzo

Copyright © 2020 Dr Shannon Panzo
All rights reserved.
March 2020.

ISBN-13: 978-0-6487848-0-7

CHAPTER 1 — 1

Consciousness is Self-Awareness — 1

- "When it Rains, it Pours!" — 3
  - Individual Consciousness — 4
  - Weather Control — 4
- Real World Value — 6
  - As the Owl flies by at night, do you hear the call? — 9
  - Money Consciousness — 11
- Common Belief vs. Individual Belief — 13
- Consciousness is being Self Aware — 13
- Just a Pipe Dream? — 13
- Your Powerful Mind (Consciousness) — 15
- Your Personal Consciousness – The Light Bulb Effect — 15
  - What Can You Do About it? — 16
  - Quantum Leaps and Insights — 16
- Giants Unite to Raise Human Consciousness — 17
  - Dr Edgar Mitchell – VP Educom (Past) — 19
  - Richard Welch, PhD — 20

CHAPTER 2 — 21

Global Consciousness — 21

- Global Consciousness - Change Becomes Abstract — 22
- Ripples in the Pond – Causality — 24
- The Consciousness of Time - Holding Stasis — 27
- Are telomeres the tell-tale signs of time consciousness tampering? — 29
- The Awareness of the Great Unwashed - Switched Off — 31
- The New Magic is Science — 31
- Vindicating Miracles as True Miracles — 32
  - SECRET DOCUMENT: "Relationships with Inhabitants Of Celestial Bodies." — 34
- Quantum Physics - Relationships of Energy and Frequency on Communication — 36
- Consciousness, Quantum Physics, and Communication — 37
- A Double-Edged Sword — 39
  - When did the Global Consciousness become Rigid? — 39
  - Communication is instantaneous - Quantum Entanglement — 40
- The Hundredth Monkey Effect — 42
  - Results of experiment triggers other observations elsewhere — 43
  - The Hundredth Monkey Effect is commonly misunderstood — 44

References: (Hundredth Monkey Effect)	46
"Skeptic Earth" – The Oroborus Effect	47
Intellectuals' Edict: - The Crucible Against Change	48

CHAPTER 3 — 49

Photographic Memory — 49

Photographic Memory - The Holy Grail of Brain Development	50
What is the Photographic Memory?	50
Photographic Memory and Global Consciousness	52
The Photographic Memory - Hollywood Creates Impossible Expectations	53
HSAM (Highly Superior Autobiographical Memory)	53
Why do most people abandon their photographic memory?	57
Your photographic memory is exercised and used every day.	58

CHAPTER 4 — 60

Global Consciousness Universal Consciousness — 60

Differences between Global Consciousness and Universal Consciousness	61
Sudden Insight - Invention	61

CHAPTER 5 — 63

Departure into the Abyss As Heaven Unfolds — 63

Multiverse	64

CHAPTER 6 — 67

Exit The Ordinary — 67

Departure to Cryptozoology and Forbidden Archaeology in this dimension	68
Multiverse Threatens Stability of Global Consciousness	68
Imagine This, to Infinity and Beyond...	69
Draconis Invertis - Dragons vs. Dinosaurs	71

CHAPTER 7 — 73

Repercussions — 73

Boomerang Effect - Life Threatening Repercussions	74

Magnetism - Unlimited Power Source	77
Ley Lines...	77
Ancient Wisdom Carried Over for Modern Applications	78
Right and Wrong Ways to Apply Obelisks	79
Good Scientists Never let Subtleties get in the Way of Progress.	81
The "Philadelphia Experiment" - Lesson NOT Learned...	82
Reports regarding the Large Hadron Collider at CERN...	84
Trust Your Government to Protect You, ... From the Truth?	84
Localized Effects of Magnetic Fields, Ley Lines, and Magnetic Anomalies...	85
Ley Lines, Vortexes, 3-D Portals (x, y, z), and 4-D Portals (x, y, z, t)...	86
Doorways and Portals...	89
Why does interdimensional activity concentrate in magnetically charged areas?	91
Use Your Senses to Detect Co-Habitation	92
No Good Deed (Honesty) Goes Unpunished...	92

CHAPTER 8   94

Confusione Ascensionem   94

Ascension	95
Ascension as Spiritual Enlightenment	96
Ascension and Transformation	96
Global / Mass Ascension - The Past is the Antithesis	96
Previous Pasts [2, 3, 4...] Cause Inconsistencies; Cast Doubt on the Present	98
Curiosity Kills a Cat?	99
When Old School Meets New School Bureaucracy	99
Implementation of Confusing Benchmarks Set Stage - Mandela Effect	100
Personal Ascension - Giant Step in Your Spiritual Enlightenment	101

CHAPTER 9   103

Regarding Hope   103

APPENDICES   106

References	107
Article 1	109
New Vision With Weather – When It Rains, It Pours	109
Appendix I	115
Continuation of United Nations Report...	115

Chapter 1
Consciousness is Self-Awareness

An Exercise in Self Discovery

"Alice's Adventures in Wonderland" - *Lewis Carroll, 1865*

Like "Alice in Wonderland", the further you go into "Wonderland", many unimaginable things happen. Some are bright new realities. Sometimes new and unique problems occur, for which just as imaginative solutions must be found. Eventful like life, Wonderland, although having its rewards, is not always a feel-good place, where everything is nice. It can be dangerous at times. The "impossible" can be made real. As the story unfolds, it has a parallel to life. It could very well represent an alternate dimension to this one.

Welcome to the "Rabbit hole".

The definition of ...
consciousness
'kɒnʃəsnɪs/
noun

1 - the state of being aware of and responsive to one's surroundings.
Synonyms: awareness, wakefulness, alertness, responsiveness, sentience

2 - a person's awareness or perception of something.
synonyms: awareness of, mindfulness of, perception of, apprehension of, recognition of

Even though we can define the word, it still does not express all of the meanings that it bestows onto other expressions and concepts.

Consciousness, as a word, has many different meanings. The deeper you go, the further you reach. Plumb the depths of your reality.

"When it Rains, it Pours!"

Your consciousness has the ability to reach into uncharted areas and perform amazing tasks. A while ago I wrote an article about an unusual way of thinking applied to every day occurrences with profound results. This article first appeared at:

https://mindtomind.com/weather-when-it-rains-it-pours/
This article appears at the end of the book under Article 1

Your consciousness affects everything you do, everything you are and will ever be. You cannot separate yourself from it. It is as cohesive as your life force is. It is interwoven into the fabric of your creation. Therefore, your consciousness can create by accessing that intrinsic connection time and again.

Individual Consciousness

Each person exists within a 'paradigm'. Your paradigm is very private. It is a relative box of your reality. It represents your limitations and is the way you perceive your world; and your consciousness is your perception and awareness as to how you interact with that world. It also represents your part of the Holographic Universe.

Your consciousness affects your world and the worlds of other individuals. Why am I saying worlds? To each individual, their world, viewed from within their paradigm, is somewhat different to the next person. Thus, each of us sees the world differently.

How much impact do you believe you have upon your world? The answer will surprise you. We will explore many causal effects as you progress through this work..

Weather Control

Governments are not the only entities that can control the weather. Born of legends, weather control has always been a part of shamanic ritual. A Shaman of a tribe will coordinate the direction of focus for the tribe to achieve a single prosperous goal – Rain! By extending the individual conscious into like-mindedness with others in a singular direction, we move our Holographic Universe to provide that which will ease our burden, and give us what we need in life; and sometimes for life to exist at all.

Today, people often believe, "It always rains when I wash my car Just like a prophecy; the skies may be clear without a cloud in sight. As you begin to wash your car, the clouds gather, seemingly from nowhere. By the time you are finished, the first drops of rain are smacking on the freshly polished surface of your car. Is this a self-fulfilling prophecy, or has your subconscious manoeuvered you to suffer your belief? Only your subconscious knows the correct answer.

DISCUSSION: Your belief in how an event should unfold often foretells the result of the event. Therefore, if you change your belief in the unfolding of the same event, then the expected result will be influenced to change, and the changed result is likely to occur. This is how you interact with the Holographic Universe.

The Holographic Universe allows you to change the configuration of the world around you. If you don't like the picture, you can replace it with a different picture. This reacts for both good and bad. By understanding you provide the input, gives you control over the resulting 'picture'. The analogy of the 'picture' used here represents all the facets of your life.

What if you rode a motorcycle everywhere? When it is raining, you would expect to get wet. What if you could ride a motorcycle while raining, and not get wet? After attending my seminar, a client programmed, "When riding my motorcycle in the rain, it can rain all around me, not on me, and the road in front of me will always be clear and dry. For years, he rode in the rain without getting wet. When last I heard from him, it was still the same. This is a good example of directly affecting your Holographic Universe.

It is much easier to do this to affect a single person, but things get complicated when doing it for more than one. It is much easier to affect one paradigm than to affect multiple paradigms, unless all paradigms involved are in harmonious agreement for exactly the same intended result. Thus, the Shaman has the tribe focus their attention on 1 anticipated result. The Shaman is also responsible for the day to day welfare of the tribe. This increases his personal influence with others, to create full belief in the outcomes the tribe pursues. The strength of each individual can be focused and added to the whole to achieve specific objectives.

Real World Value

5% of the people control 95% of the wealth of this planet. That means that 95% of the people on the planet are fighting over the remaining 5%. Today, we still live in the same world that we lived in before – 50 years ago.. The inherent resources and wealth distribution have stayed relatively the same. Starting with 1968, 5% still controlled 95% of the world's wealth. But there were only 3.6 Billion people on the planet to share the 5%. Now there are 7.6 Billion people – more than twice as many people in only 50 years, to share relatively the same 5% of the wealth.

Is it any wonder why so many people are suffering "lack" today, that were not suffering lack years ago? We have more than **doubled the world population in less than 50 years!**

Significant people are in closed-door discussions about how to curb, or even cull, humans to reverse the population growth down to sustainable numbers. If you don't think it is happening, think again. For point of reference, Google: "United Nations population control". The absence of official documentation is not really a surprise. Google was probably ordered to expunge the information. For such a wide reaching Global issue, there does not appear to be much news at all. Awareness is often the result of looking for the important things NOT talked about.

How does this type of real input affect an individual person's consciousness? Do you think it may add stress? Some people would love to go back and to live in the 1950s. Of course it seemed so much easier back then... because it WAS easier.

World Population (Last 50 Years)

Year	World Population
2020	7,794,798,739 (estimate)
2019	7,713,468,100
2010	6,956,823,603
2000	6,143,493,823
1990	5,327,231,061
1980	4,458,003,514
1970	3,700,437,046
1968	3,551,599,127

Courtesy of WorldoMeters.info/world-population/world-population-by-year/ - Dover, DE, USA

FYI: The United Nations' Dynamic Report Regarding Sustainability

The United Nations published a report while this book was in draft form. The report is included for your information. It is unusual that the UN would take such a stance without significant reason.

IMPORTANT NOTE: *Please take into account that there are as many agendas as there are contributors to the data compiled here. Some (or much) of the information expressed in the report can be considered controversial and contradictory to the absolute facts. Only you can decide how this information affects your personal consciousness. If you already use Mental Photography for assimilating information, please use it to scan the report to distinguish the truth for yourself. I have included the entire report as Appendix I at the end of the book.*

Topics absent from the United Nations report include, but are not limited to:
- Volcanic activity – impact on greenhouse gases
- Other natural sources and phenomena impacting greenhouse gasses
- Sun – radiation from the Solar Cycle impacting global temperatures and weather – Even though certain relationships have been observed with weather patterns, these phenomena can neither be confirmed nor denied relative to temperature only.
- Impact of weather control (HAARP) and other such technology.
- Although "Socialism" is omitted, there are key references to "social" dynamics, partially due to pre-existing agenda of the United Nations.

May 6, 2019: The United Nations report on non-sustainability of resources and mass extinctions looming...

PARIS, 6 May – Nature is declining globally at rates unprecedented in human history – and the rate of species extinctions is accelerating, with grave impacts on people around the world now likely, warns a landmark new report from the Intergovernmental Science-Policy Platform on Biodiversity and Ecosystem Services (IPBES), the summary of which was approved at the 7th session of the IPBES Plenary, meeting last week (29 April – 4 May) in Paris.

(The Article in full is included at the end of the book as Appendix I.)

(Information provided above is excerpted from the following United Nations Internet page: https://www.un.org/sustainabledevelopment/blog/2019/05/nature-decline-unprecedented-report/)

As the Owl flies by at night, do you hear the call?

Stephen Hawking, one of the world's most renowned speakers, gave much consideration to the global overpopulation issue and how it will influence the world in the future.

"We are in danger of destroying ourselves by our greed and stupidity. We cannot remain looking inwards at ourselves on a small and increasingly polluted and overcrowded planet" – Stephen Hawking

"Our population and our use of the finite resources of planet Earth are growing exponentially, along with our technical ability to change the environment for good or ill" – Stephen Hawking

"Life on Earth is at the ever-increasing risk of being wiped out by a disaster, such as sudden global nuclear war, a genetically engineered virus or other dangers we have not yet thought of" – Stephen Hawking

Some may say Stephen is the bearer of bad news, and some would say he is planting the seed for those who would intentionally destroy this world. In any case, his opinion is based in the current facts we are forced to face. It is up to you to decide what this knowledge means to you.

In the past, another person of great intellect, **Nicola Tesla**, Inventor (1856 – 1943), was raised in a strict religious environment of high integrity, at a time when a person's word actually meant something. As he observed trouble brewing on the horizon, his harsh words add gravity to some clearly defined problems the world has accumulated and multiplied over time by nullifying the 'natural selection' of the gene pool.

"The year 2100 will see eugenics universally established. In past ages, the law governing the survival of the fittest roughly weeded out the less desirable strains. Then man's new sense of pity began to

interfere with the ruthless workings of nature. As a result, **we continue to keep alive and to breed the unfit**. *The only method compatible with our notions of civilization and the race is to prevent the breeding of the unfit by sterilization and the deliberate guidance of the mating instinct, Several European countries and a number of states of the American Union sterilize the criminal and the insane. This is not sufficient. The trend of opinion among eugenicists is that we must make marriage more difficult. Certainly no one who is not a desirable parent should be permitted to produce progeny. A century from now it will no more occur to a normal person to mate with a person eugenically unfit than to marry a habitual criminal"* — *Nikola Tesla*

Nicola Tesla thought he had it right. Humanity was emerging from the cesspool of labor intensive early days, when the value of life was insignificant; unless you were lucky enough to be born privileged. Tesla believed humanity was embarking on a "Golden Age" of invention, enlightenment, morality, and integrity, and the interactions between people would grow in honor and sincerity.

What he did not imagine was the world would be craving what they had left behind; the forbidden fruit of decadence, debauchery, and self-degradation. Morality and integrity, all but forgotten. Innocence is lost. Look to the politicians for answers about the decay of society and the corruption of wholesome family values, and why special interest groups reign supreme over the majority. Nicola Tesla was a true idealist. He died in a New York City Hotel, alone and impoverished.

Are we paying for the crimes of our ancestors? Ignorance is no excuse. Just because it makes people uncomfortable to discuss certain things is good reason such topics should be revisited by the governments which have created the problems in the first place. Fairness and equality is for everyone ... or for none.

"antisocial behavior is a trait of intelligence in a world of conformists." — *Nikola Tesla*

Money Consciousness

People with plenty of money and wealth, do not tend to worry about money at all. Since they believe it will always be there by their experience, it just seems it always falls that way, with few exceptions.

People who are not wealthy seem to always be worried about where their next dollar is coming from. In other words, their conscious mind is always focused on the "lack" of wealth. Therefore, if a person focuses all their thoughts about wealth on "lack", then that is what they will attract more of – lack.

There has been more stress on lack multiplied by all the media increasing their audience based revenue at your expense. When you combine with the population growth chart showing how the accessible wealth is less than half there was 50 years ago, you can easily see why people are feeling it.

Any time there is something that will make people feel poor, it makes for great news. Then as others reiterate what they have heard through media, it further multiplies. This type of negative thinking robs your consciousness of the good things that happen all the time. Strategically, fasten hold of the good events happening around you. They will anchor you to the right frequency.

Meditation and personal programming are the means to install goodness into your life, so it takes root and assists you to combat the negative trends that others were duped into believing through unintended acquiescence.

NOTE: Instead of programming for the amount of money intended to fulfil a desired result, I suggest my clients program on the result instead. Money is a trap. If you treat it as such and leave it out of your programming, then your programming is not dependent on it. Taking this approach increases your awareness to the false values most people place upon money.

If you are having a bad hair day ... perhaps you are just trying a different style.

NOTES

Common Belief vs. Individual Belief

If everyone around you appears to think the same way about a topic, does it mean you must agree with that way of thinking as well? Perhaps the appearance that all the people think the same way is an illusion. A number of those people are only agreeing through acquiescence. (They accept your silence as you agreeing, yes.)

POINT: Political Correctness often uses this strategy to get people to appear to be agreeing, because people are fearful of making a stand against what is said. **Political Correctness breeds fear, hatred, and discontent.** *The only way to combat this is to attack Political Correctness directly; as a corruption of ideals for support of false agendas. The truth is always the truth.*

You are an individual. In most cases, you can express your differences without threat to life or limb. You may find that many others agree with you – more than the false consensus. Those others are weak and too insecure to believe in themselves. While in this state of weakness, the person is severely limited by their paradigm and the holographic universe. The chance they could change either is negligible.

Consciousness is being Self Aware

Your consciousness is expressed as self-awareness. To be aware of the world around you, and interact with that world, your Holographic Universe; then you can choose to change it. You can toss out the things you don't like and bring into reality the things you do want. Why not? You have already been interacting with it all of your life. You were not aware of it before.

Just a Pipe Dream?

At this point you may be thinking, "Shannon, that is all very well. But, how does it involve me? It sounds like a pipe dream."

Quantum Physicists since Albert Einstein's day must have been smoking a lot of something. If you follow the basic principles of Quantum Physics, it is science that has grown to respect that many things happen in space and time that are not clearly accounted for by using hard crunched mathematics.

Today we are aware of many things that exist in this one plane of existence, where at the time this is written, there have been at least 22 more planes discovered that overlay the plane you are in; like overlapping pages of the same book.

Everything is constructed of chaotic energy; every energy, frequency, waveform, subatomic particle, and the relationships between them. The only thing that seemingly holds it all together is a universal intelligence that an atom remembers what form it took yesterday, and today, and decides to remain that atom tomorrow.

From certain experiments that have been conducted and observed, there is proof that there is some form of communication that is instantaneous throughout the cosmos. It is not encumbered by time nor distance.

This special "glue" that literally holds the universe together has a few interesting properties that our limited mental abilities can come to terms with.
- Instantaneous communication anywhere within the Universe. (All Knowing)
- Intelligence expressed in everything (Omnipotent)
- ...and it has been there since the beginning of time (Alpha and Omega)

Quantum Physics has discovered the essence of what has only been held in religion as truth.

> *"If you want to find the secrets of the Universe, think in terms of energy, frequency, and vibration."* — Nikola Tesla

Your Powerful Mind (Consciousness)

Your mind has the power within to create, influence, and change energy into matter. You are the master of the many things in motion around you once you become familiarized with this way of thinking and doing. When you become adept at orchestrating the movement, controlling things like the weather becomes child's play. Remember, you are first influencing your personal space – the space that only you should have control over.

Your Personal Consciousness – The Light Bulb Effect

You have just discovered you are not limited by what you have learned or heard from others. You are not limited by your surroundings. You are not limited by any rules, regulations, or anything else of substance. You are not even limited by time and space! So, what are you going to do?

The aperture of this huge awareness is closing and you have not made a decision. It is new information. You do not know whether to trust it, or to play it safe and reject it. At this very moment, you hold sway over time itself, but you cannot sit on the fence. You must make a decision.

There! The decision was made for you. Time has expired. You can play it safe, as you always have. Don't worry. Even though you have been exposed to this information, most people are just like you. When it comes to the crunch, especially a decision with such finality, they refer back to what they know – safe harbor. <u>Your life will never be the same again.</u>

What Can You Do About it?

Now that you know it really is there, you can expand your awareness, and take some time to familiarize yourself with the concepts. You can still grow your awareness and consciousness. You can still influence your world and the Holographic Universe, and you can still create things to happen in a preferred way.

When you expand your awareness / consciousness, you see, feel, smell, hear, and taste more as all of your senses are switched on. You begin to experience your 6th sense, ESP, at an all-new level you have not experienced before. It was always there, but you were not really hooked up to it; gaining the benefits.

As your consciousness expands, you can take control and influence your world to unfold in the way you want. People around you will also change. Since you have changed, you are sending out a different frequency. Sometimes that frequency is disharmonious with the people you have known for a long time. They react as they see you a stranger to them – an outsider. Their path through life may not be the same as yours – the fork in the road.

Quantum Leaps and Insights

As your Consciousness continues to grow, you will automatically learn to accept that you are moving onto higher ground. To you, the changes will feel insignificant, except for the "Aha!" moments, where you get an insight. Your newfound energy will attract new friends, wanting to know this new person joining their ranks. It is just another progression as you move through life.

Your personal consciousness connects you with many ideals and insights, Global Consciousness, Universal Consciousness, even connecting you with other dimensions, as you feel that something is there, just out of touch. Time is not immune to your influence. Time is more than time "flying" when you are having fun, or time "dragging on" when you are bored, or doing something you don't want to do.

You can influence time to change. The first proof this happens was when the first Astronauts were in space. When they returned back to earth, the chronographs had lost ~3 minutes. If time was static as we are led to believe, then that would not have occurred. Once the astronauts left the gravity of Earth and influence of the Global Consciousness, those things no longer confined time at the same rate as on Earth.

This account was given to us by Dr. Edgar Mitchell, Apollo 14 Astronaut, 6th man recorded to step onto the Moon. Dr. Mitchell founded IONS, and was the Vice President for Market Development for Brain Management (Educom, Inc). He conducted documented telepathic testing between the moon and his testing team on Earth, and found that telepathy was possible and the results were instantaneous.

Giants Unite to Raise Human Consciousness

As the Founder of the Institute of Noetic Science, Dr Mitchell sought out all manner of Gurus, Teachers, and Mental Disciplines from around the world – to observe and evaluate them for advancements in enlightenment and raising the consciousness of humans.

After researching these Gurus, and Mental Disciplines from all over the world, Dr. Mitchell sought to be involved with Brain Management and ongoing efforts with Dr Richard Welch. He found the Brain

Management approach and results unique when compared to other mind disciplines. Dr Mitchell found that Brain Management and Mental Photography; by utilizing natural brain function and applications of the photographic memory, was superior for many reasons. *"It bridges the gap between logical deduction and spontaneous creation. **The missing Guru's How To Training."***

While working with **Dr Richard Welch, "the Father of Mental Photography",** Dr Mitchell provided his extended insights to Brain Management Instructors and staff. The Brain Management training attracts people who want to explore their abilities, push themselves past their mental limitations, and raise their consciousness.

Dr Edgar Mitchell – VP Educom (Past)

*"Mental Photography...
is
light years beyond reading or speed reading,
...it is like looking back at the Earth From the Moon"*

"Learning the ability to accurately absorb and retain vast quantities of pertinent information is itself a remarkable feat which assures increasing one's confidence, self-esteem and marketability. But learning how to relax and manage stress naturally provides a ten-fold increase in benefit for Mental Photographers. What better way to be of service to our fellow humans and to simultaneously create a better life for ourselves than to introduce everyone to the benefits of Brain Management® (ZOX Pro) System?"

– Dr. Edgar Mitchell

– Apollo 14 Astronaut, Founder of Institute of Noetic Sciences (IONS)
– Past Vice President of Brain Management (Educom, Inc) ZOX Pro

Richard Welch, PhD

"The more we know about the brain, the more we realise how little we know."

"Father of Mental Photography"
CEO – EDUCOM Brain Management (ret.)

Since 1975, Dr Richard Welch was led to discover many great things with regards to learning and how the brain functions. His most noteworthy discovery is Mental Photography – the ability to access the photographic memory at rates beginning at 25,000 words per minute and higher, with 100% retention of the information for life.

Mental Photography is the Holy Grail for learning and exercising the brain.

Welcome to Tomorrow!

Chapter 2
Global Consciousness

Global Consciousness - Change Becomes Abstract

Photo by Skeeze / Pixabay

There is a tree growing in a field, alive and breathing. Over time, we see other trees sprout up around the first. They are the same type of tree. Where did they come from? The new trees are extensions of the first tree, growing from the roots of the original tree.

Consciousness acts this way. Once one idea or ideal is created in the consciousness, it expands in its awareness to create more of the same type of knowledge. Eventually the first tree grows into its own forest, like consciousness spreads outwards to affect the Global Consciousness.

Therefore, once an idea, left unchallenged, catches hold, then it spreads throughout the global consciousness. Once that idea becomes a static part of the global consciousness, it is nearly impossible to repeal, or modify the idea, even if it is flawed or invalid.

Before, I spoke about individual awareness and your consciousness. You have the ability to make an incredible impact upon your personal environment. Imagine the incredible amount of change we could effect when Global Consciousness is the driving force behind change.

Perhaps the clouds can be the color of orange sherbet and the raindrops made of golden Manna providing our every need. Oh yes, you can dream.

NOTES

Ripples in the Pond – Causality

Image by Arek Socha / Pixabay

Your individual consciousness is like tossing a single pebble into a still pond. The ripples spread out in all directions. The influence of one can change everything. Your personal influence is infinite.

Adding another person with their own individual consciousness, they too toss a pebble into the pond. Depending on their pebble's position to your pebble, it can interfere with the ripples - achieving a result neither person was wanting, strengthening the ripples - assisting with the changes, but may modify the result, or opposing your ripples - possibly cancelling the effect of both pebbles entirely. The result would be based on the different perception and preferred result from both people instead of only the one person.

Today, there are more than 7.6 Billion pebbles hitting the surface. Each individual has impact, but the collaborative result is becoming less and less specific. The resulting effect is chaotic - as a wave results, or it is insignificant.- as all the pebbles nullify the efforts to nil - stasis. In terms of Global Consciousness, there are some properties that are static, and people have accepted it. This acceptance is broadcast even at a cellular level, that certain things cannot change; even when there is proof otherwise.

Many things that are held static in the Global Consciousness, can be changed, but the general consensus is not to attempt to change them. In an individual consciousness, change can be triggered by a crisis, as well as self-implied direction. Therefore the scale of crisis to change things for Global Consciousness would be catastrophic. Typical examples of this would be:

> The extinction of the dinosaurs
> Volcanos such as Mount Vesuvius, Krakatoa / Krakatau, and the potential Yellowstone super-volcano at Yellowstone National Park in Wyoming, Montana, and Idaho, USA. (Volcanoes: 2018 = 72, 2019 = 64+)
> Earthquakes, tsunamis, and other titanic earth-shaking events that are felt around the world

[NOTE: Although wars are full of crisis and felt globally, they are often sullied by agenda and constructed as a means of taking power from others. They can also be used as a means of forced depopulation or to conduct genocide of targeted groups of people. Since wars can be created by human intervention, I am not including them here, as this would give credence that they are somehow natural events that cannot be prevented.]

Upcoming Crises that will automatically change Global Consciousness:
> When the Global Population vs. Resources threshold is exceeded
> Pandemics (plagues)
> ...many other events have high potential

Images by:
**Skeeze
StockSnap
Enriquelopezgarre
at Pixabay**

The Consciousness of Time - Holding Stasis

"Time is an Illusion" - Albert Einstein

Quantum scientists understand that time does not exist the same for every place, person, or situation: instead, it is created and held in stasis as a creation of global consciousness by most of the people on the planet. In other words, as quantum physicists indicate, *"Time is a creation of the human mind"*, and *"All time exists within a single moment."*

DISCUSSION: We are dealing with two very polarized concepts based upon unrelated parameters. The only constant between the two is your consciousness. The first concept is that global consciousness holds time in stasis due to the steadfast belief of humanity. The second concept from quantum physics is that all time occurs simultaneously. Intrinsically in this model; time, as we perceive it, ceases to exist - evaporating into the ether of cosmic consciousness. Only you can determine what is real for you.

"The separation between past, present, and future is only an illusion" Albert Einstein

"The only reason for time is so that everything does not happen at once." Albert Einstein

"one of the twins went for a long trip in a spaceship at nearly the speed of light. When he returned, he would be much younger than the one who stayed on earth. This is known as the twins paradox, but it is a paradox only if one has the idea of absolute time at the back of one's mind. In the theory of relativity there is no unique absolute time, but instead each individual has his own personal measure of time that depends on where he is and how he is moving."
— Stephen Hawking, A Brief History of Time

The result of the illusion of time being a product of the human mind in turn applies all the limitations to the entire planet, and is directed into our Holographic Universe. As an individual, you can accept or deny time as static when you consider this within your own individual consciousness and personal holographic universe.

NOTES

Are telomeres the tell-tale signs of time consciousness tampering?

You may wonder how far reaching the imposed time-consciousness affects can be. Within your genetic structure, your DNA, there are 'time fragments' called telomeres.

In your genetic coding, as your cells replicate, the telomeres break off; timing down the effective life of the cell. Cells get old and die, and are replaced by fresh new cells - in an ideal world. Whenever the cell runs out of the fragments to break off, it can no longer divide to make new cells.. This is also referred to as the aging process.

Unfortunately, not all cells are replaced, and the older cells may come under stress and fall victim to disease. Leading up to the end of the person's life, is typically not a comfortable nor idyllic set of events. Telomeres are not limited to humans. They are found in a wide range of eukaryotic species, from humans to single-cell organisms.

Likewise, if the telomeres did not break off, you would stay young, healthy, and vibrant - and death may become something that is not of the normal existence. The implied stress to your consciousness would not exist, so there would be great joy in living life. The benefits are twofold, as one of the top precursors to premature aging is stress.

Is the existence of telomeres at the most basic level of our genetic code the reason why it is easy to 'buy in' that time is static, or are the telomeres a product of forced evolution brought upon by global consciousness imposing the will of most people to bear onto your individual consciousness? This is the time we must ask which came first? The chicken or the egg? Global consciousness or telomeres?

There is hope! Scientists all over the world have been finding ways to slow, even stop the breakage, rebuild the telomeres, and even refresh old cells into young cells, creating new telomeres in the process. Achieving those things could stop the clock ticking, and perhaps stop, or even reverse the aging process. This will provide momentum for you to change your perception and application of time within your personal holographic universe.

The Fountain of Youth is at Hand

NOTES

The Awareness of the Great Unwashed - Switched Off

Billions of people mill about, going about their daily activities, without perceiving there is anything they can do to change their existence. Their awareness of paradigms, their individual consciousness, or the effect of global consciousness on their lives is simply outside of their perspective. Yet they are the fulcrum point as to time, or any other ideal, being static in the holographic universe created and maintained by the global consciousness.

Is there really anyone to blame for such an obvious atrocity? Not really. It just crept up on us. We were complacent. In the early days, we did not see the signs, because we did not know what to look for. Hindsight is 20/20.

There would have been a time when the Mystics understood that by incorporating a tribe, or a number of people, into a cooperating group to seek the same end, they were able to stretch and bend reality of a more localised version of the global consciousness to achieve that end. There would not have been enough specific fact, like the Laws of Physics, conflicting to the outcome that would have prevented it. Over time, with population growth and hardened facts, those same ideas would be nearly impossible to achieve.

The New Magic is Science

Today, the global consciousness cannot control the newest discoveries; many made by quantum physicists. Since these discoveries are kept relatively secret, the fabric of space and time can be stretched and folded to influence these findings because the balance point within the global consciousness has not yet been achieved. Many of these advanced concepts are simply outside of the intellectual reach of all except the most adept. Until those incredible discoveries come out of the shadows and into the light of day, or from the realm of magic into reality, the perception of the ideas won't be static within global consciousness.

Due to the secret nature of the findings, the evidence that such things are already in existence is simply not at hand. Again, that is why it is referred to as "Secret". Rest assured, the top scientists and the military have access to more than the few "weird scientific discoveries" I have indicated here.

Vindicating Miracles as True Miracles

PERHAPS... this is the reason the pyramids were built without a suitable explanation in modern thinking, or how Moses was able to part the Red Sea with "God's Hand" to open the way. *(Global population at the time of Moses was ~40M. I estimate the population in the regions of the Nile, Tigris, and Euphrates Rivers would not have come near the number of people living in New York City today. People during that time would have scattered settlements, but would mainly congregate around the largest cities.)*

There are many other ancient miracles listed all over the world from many civilizations. Today, we cannot perceive how these miracles were achieved without the modern technology we have today. Some cannot be achieved, even with modern technology.

"I expect Miracles to Happen Daily" **- Dr Shannon Panzo**

Since most people on Earth don't believe time can be modified in any way, their combined global consciousness holds time in stasis. Time is a construct; a fabrication of our own consciousness on a grand scale.

Previously, I mentioned the first Astronauts needing to reset their chronographs upon returning to Earth, proving Einstein's observations that time is flexible based on other parameters such as gravity. One of the effects is referred to as **"time dilation"**. Here is one of the most recognised representations shown here:

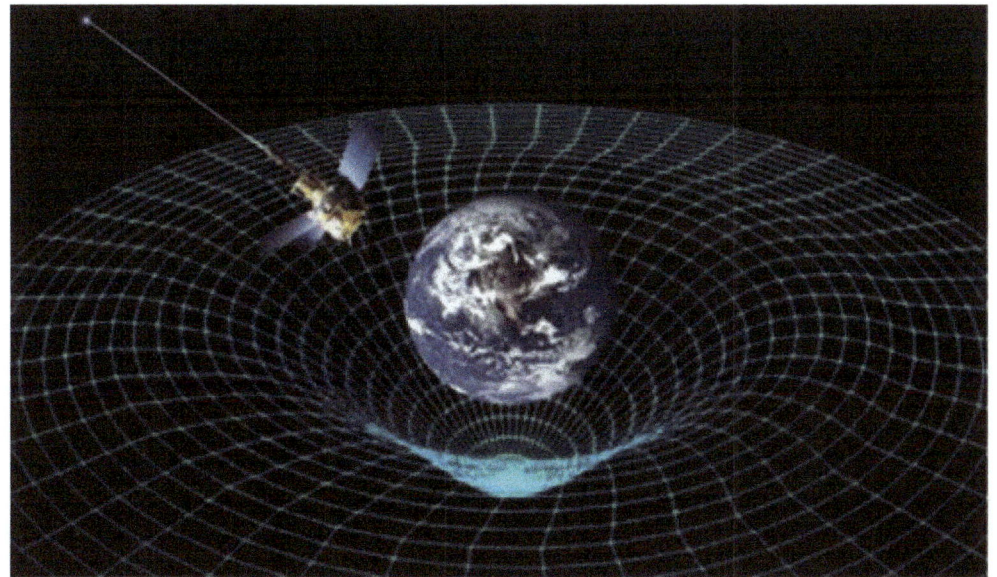

Image credit: NASA

Time Dilation - This represents Earth's gravity affecting the fabric of time/space. Differences in time dilation is due to the mass and gravity of planets to the fabric of space/time.

The Extraterrestrial Enigma Revealed - Bad Karma for Global Consciousness

I always find it amazing how much important, Earth-shattering information is withheld from public view. We live in the age of smoke and mirrors, with the main players being the government and the media organizations. They propagate images that falsely strengthen lies, further contaminating the global consciousness. An obvious example of this type of smokescreen cover-up still used today is all about extraterrestrial life and UFOs.

It is unknown who quoted this first... *"If the accumulated body of evidence supporting the existence of extraterrestrials and UFOs were submitted to a court of law, there would be no hesitation to convict."*

Scientists have often commented about and around the subject of UFOs and Extraterrestrials. In 1920, Albert Einstein asked, *"Why should earth be the only planet supporting human life?"*

SECRET DOCUMENT: "Relationships with Inhabitants Of Celestial Bodies."

Einstein and Oppenheimer wrote a formal document in 1947, "Relationships With Inhabitants Of Celestial Bodies." At the time it was top secret, but now it is declassified. The document was only six pages long but what it does say is incredible. It claims that the presence of <u>UFOs is something the military accepted a long time ago</u>. The document talks about what actions should be taken in the event of aliens coming to our planet. One brilliant quote from the document is this, *"If these intelligent beings were in possession of a more or less culture, and a more or less perfect political organization, they would have an absolute right to be recognized as independent and sovereign peoples, we would have to come to* *an agreement with them to establish the legal regulations upon which future relationships should be based, and it would be necessary to accept many of their principles."* It was advised that such information be withheld from the public, because the ramifications would have terrible consequences.

Imagine if that became public opinion in 1947, and how that one idea would have made massive changes to the global consciousness, forever! Perhaps, ever since that time there have been plenty of movies and stories to indoctrinate us into the eventual mass discovery, when the governments can no longer cover it up. Even now, most people believe that intelligent extraterrestrial life exists.

In 2010, Stephen Hawking said, *"If aliens visit us, the outcome would be much as when Columbus landed in America, which didn't turn out well for the Native Americans."*

Summary: Public disclosure of the facts are imperative to the support of a healthy global consciousness. If the global conscious is supported with lies and non-disclosure of facts, is it any wonder that most people automatically lie instead of facing the truth? This eroded perspective is passed down from the global consciousness into your individual consciousness, making it a strong temptation. It is only strong-willed people that see the merit of truth, and the rewards in honoring the truth.

Quantum Physics - Relationships of Energy and Frequency on Communication

Quantum physicists report that everything is a construct from the chaotic energy, the "stuff" the universe is made of.

I want to bring into this a quote from Stephen Hawking to highlight the idea that it is not just the cosmic soup that is everything everywhere, but also the interaction this energy has with our consciousness - our mind...

"How do I know that a table still exists if I go out of the room and can't see it? What does it mean to say that things we can't see, such as electrons or quarks—the particles that are said to make up the proton and neutron—exist? One could have a model in which the table disappears when I leave the room and reappears in the same position when I come back, but that would be awkward, and what if something happened when I was out, like the ceiling falling in? How, under the table-disappears-when-I-leave-the-room model, could I account for the fact that the next time I enter, the table reappears broken, under the debris of the ceiling? The model in which the table stays put is much simpler and agrees with observation. That is all one can ask." - *Stephen Hawking*

To extrapolate this a bit further. Your computer does not exist until you see it in front of you. Even though you went through the motions of spending the money at the store to acquire it in the first place, only because that is what you expected to do to obtain the computer. You even made the trip to the store because it was what you expected to do.

Therefore, the entire Internet lay open before you, as you access it, with the infinitely oppressive amount of data that is there for you, but until the moment you gained access it did not exist - neither did the billions of other users now seemingly accessing and creating the information you previously did not have access to... Or did you? Essentially, you created the entire Internet upon the whim of accessing it. This is how the Holographic Universe is felt. It represents many things, including your control over it.

Your consciousness constructs your world in front of you, step by step. It is easy to look back at your past. All time is simultaneous. There are no hard and fast rules. Seeing the future is difficult because the future is based on your consciousness reconstructing future events and actions created from your decisions, no matter how infinitesimally small they seem to be.

SUMMARY: You may be confused at this point. That is fine. This may be the first time you ever heard this information. It is perfectly fine if you continue to think it to be nonsense. That is what you have chosen to do. Your consciousness will fill in the gaps seamlessly. Pay attention to the way you think and feel as you wind your way through this information. Your mind may be revealing more to you than what you consider possible.

Consciousness, Quantum Physics, and Communication

Everything you see, hear, smell, touch, taste, and more, are forms of communication. They all have their intrinsic nature in "star stuff" - energy and frequency. Your observations, the conversations you have, the things you read, the information you consume - types of communication; all are created from that same substance of chaotic energy.

Start with something you can relate to - the words you read. A single word may mean 30 different things, yet your complex mind can instantaneously assign that word the correct meaning. Your mind is so refined, it takes you less than one-third of a second to assess and pass critical judgement on a person you are meeting for the first time by looking at their face. You automatically do these things by "reading" that specific energy and highly specialized frequency by using your built-in radio receiver; your brain. Even paranormal activities such as telepathy and clairvoyance are not out of your grasp when you look at it this way.

It's hard to believe, right? At this very moment, if this is relatively new information for you, you may find your heart beat is up, perhaps a shortness of breath. A bit of a buzz is starting in your brain. Maybe you relate it to confusion, or maybe it's that niggly feeling that something has always been wrong with your world; something now revealed, something that calls out to be changed. And, if you don't have those feelings, that is perfectly fine as well.

A Double-Edged Sword

When did the Global Consciousness become Rigid?

There are two factors that have contributed the most to this "hardening" of the global consciousness. The first one is obvious. The population of the world has been steadily increasing. The second, more important contributor, is technology; mainly in the areas of communication. It wasn't until the invention of the telephone, then the television, that really triggered this to take place.

Up until then, the news was sent around using physical, nontechnical methods, such as couriers. Wars could be fought and done before you may hear about it. People in remote areas may not encounter another person for years. Story-telling of events was often embellished to make it more interesting. Hearsay became fact, no matter how ridiculous the story may be.

Finally, in the Information Age - the day of the computer, global news is only a keystroke away. Scientific evidence is easily found at hand. Rigid thinking has contributed to the hardening of the global consciousness. And yes, that includes the ideas about time and space. Only the newest secret information has escaped this encapsulation, for now.

You have inherited the limitations into your reality, as it is passed down from the global consciousness into your individual consciousness. The unknown enemy has already taken over; before you ever knew it existed. Do you still have choice - Yes!

> **"Most persons are so absorbed in the contemplation of the outside world that they are wholly oblivious to what is passing on within themselves."**
> — Nikola Tesla, My Inventions: The Autobiography of Nikola Tesla

Communication is instantaneous - Quantum Entanglement

When Dr. Edgar Mitchell performed his telepathy experiments from space, he did not need to wait for the radio signal to reach the people then have them reply back, again with a lag time between. His results were immediate, and without any hesitation.

A simple experiment in quantum physics that shows us that there is a form of communication that exists at all times in the universe, and is instantaneous, comes from what is referred to as **Quantum Entanglement** - called *"Spooky action at a distance"* by Einstein.

Quantum entanglement begins as particles are in association - perhaps electrons in the same atom. When the electrons are broken away from the atom, they spin off and travel in different directions. The speed at which they travel is at the speed of light. So, no matter what the distance is between the particles due to their adjacent angles of trajectory, if you change the direction of one of the electrons, the other electron instantly changes direction as well.

That means that the communication between the two particles is at the speed of light + X, X being an arbitrary speed based upon the trajectory of the two particles over time. If the particles are moving at 180*, then the speed would be two times the speed of light plus distance between the two increasing exponentially. The communication is still instantaneous, no matter the distance. This goes against Albert Einstein's **"Special Theory of Relativity"**; the premise that nothing can travel faster than the speed of light . Therefore, an exception has been applied to things already in motion at or beyond the speed of light.

Now, for a bit of a departure.. my "String Theory..." I observe various relationships, no matter whether they choose involvement or not. Even un-involvement may be a decision made.

Instantaneous communication between two pre-associated particles across infinite distance implies **"memory" (quantum entanglement).**

Memory implies "**intelligence**" at some unknown and basic level. This "glue" is also the decision that an atom was that atom yesterday and today, and will remain the same atom tomorrow - **choice**. Thus, you are not flying apart into chaotic energy and reassembling an infinite number of times each day... or perhaps you are?

As all time can be expressed as existing in a single moment... Einstein said, *"...us physicists believe the separation between past, present, and future is only an illusion, although a convincing one."*

Therefore, the communication/memory/intelligence has existed forever and is without end - **Alpha and Omega, Omnipotent**. It has been said that *"Science has a way of redefining religion."* Has science found God?

Image by pen_ash / Pixabay

Japanese Macaque

The Hundredth Monkey Effect

*The **hundredth monkey effect** is a hypothetical phenomenon in which a new behavior or idea is claimed to spread rapidly by unexplained means from one group to all related groups once a critical number of members of one group exhibit the new behavior or acknowledge the new idea.*

I am editorializing certain sections of the research and what has apparently happened, not happened, or potentially that could have happened...

The original Koshima research was undertaken by a team of scientists as a secondary consequence of 1948 research on semiwild horses in Japan. The Koshima troupe was identified as segregated from other monkeys and, from 1950, used as a closed study group to observe wild Japanese monkey behaviour. While studying the group the team would drop sweet potatoes and wheat on the beach and observe the troupe's behaviour. In 1954 a paper was published indicating the first observances of one monkey, Imo, washing her sweet potatoes in the water. Her changed behaviour led to several feeding behaviour changes over the course of the next few years, all of which was of great benefit in understanding the process of teaching and learning in animal behaviour.

As with most scientific experiments, only the parameters of the control and what is to be tested is what is recorded and evaluated. The scope was only on the 1 isolated tribe of monkeys and not the effect upon a global consciousness representation of that type of monkey or closely related species.

Separate papers make mention that, from 1960 onward, similar sweet potato washing behaviours were noticed in other parts of the world, however this is not directly attributed to Koshima. Claims are made that a monkey swam from one island to another where he taught the resident monkeys how to wash sweet potatoes. No mention of the other behavioural improvements are made. No indication of how the monkey swam is made either - it must be noted that the Koshima monkeys cannot swim. Therefore, although the question must be asked how the swimming monkey learned the sweet potato washing behaviour if not from Koshima, no indication is made as to where the monkey learned the behaviour.

Results of experiment triggers other observations elsewhere

After the results of the experiments were known, others began to notice similar food washing activities in other disassociated parts of the world as well. Because a global scope was not considered in the original experiment and observations, then the perceived notion that the other remote food washing came from the first set of observed monkeys could easily be discredited by logical deduction.

The Hundredth Monkey Effect is commonly misunderstood

The Hundredth Monkey Effect is NOT about the first tribe of monkeys. It is about the apparent spread of knowledge and use of the new behavior by the other tribes of monkeys having no direct contact with the first tribe.

Yes, there are potential flaws in the original testing. Since the sweet potatoes were specifically made available in such a way as to encourage a behavior, and perhaps a behavior that the tribe originally did have available, but only made use of it occasionally. (You would not want sand in your food either.) Quite possibly the other tribes of monkeys recorded 'after the fact' as having the same behavior would have it in common as a rarely used skill, or a genetic anomaly, such as what makes certain types of dogs more inclined to instinctively herd up other animals.

If the reports are true as observed, then the original premise of the Hundredth Monkey Scenario stands. Due to the remote distances between the tribes, how would all the tribes know to use this behavior in the first place? Perhaps this is actually an example of the how humans relate to time as being our static construct.

For a moment, let's assume that the Hundredth Monkey Effect can be substantiated... What part does the hundredth Monkey example play in human global consciousness? The main critical reference is the **"tipping point"**, a point in time when a group - or a large number of group members - rapidly and dramatically changes its behavior (or belief) by widely adopting a previously unknown, unused, or rare practice (or belief). This is often considered adaptability to new circumstances.

From the tribe of monkeys changing their behavior, that exists as 1/100th of all the other tribes of similar monkeys... When the other tribes of monkeys automatically appear to have sympathetically picked up and begun to use this new behavior, even when the distance between the tribes makes it impossible to rationalise any physical connection, then it can be assumed that there has been some sort of unknown connection or consciousness that has spread the behavior information to all the tribes.

You may have heard, '**it only takes 1% of the population for Earth to ascend to the next level of consciousness...**'

For global consciousness, the tipping point is considered to be 1% - the 100th Monkey. With the assumption that there is at least 50% of the population that has no predisposition in any direction to the outcome, through ignorance or otherwise, they automatically count to the positive action of the 1%, which is actually equal to the action of ~51%. This takes the new action over the critical threshold of >50% acceptance, becoming the new static belief in the consciousness. Once the 1% is met, it triggers a domino effect achieving >50%. Thus, the change is instantaneous.

Since you will never be able to convince sceptics that the Hundredth Monkey Effect is plausible, then to convince them that such ideas as taking the world into a new, elevated level of consciousness would be just as impossible. Perhaps the sceptics will be left behind in their own judgement when it does finally happen. Maybe they can inhabit "Sceptic Earth". (I sense a Sci-Fi Novel here. Sorry, no fantasy allowed. Please refer below.)

References: (Hundredth Monkey Effect)

1. b c d Amundson, Ron (Summer 1985). Kendrick Frazier, ed. "The Hundredth Monkey Phenomenon". Skeptical Inquirer: 348–356.
2. Blair, Lawrence (1975). Rhythms of Vision: The Changing Patterns of Belief. London: Croom Helm Ltd. ISBN 978-0-8052-3610-1.
3. Blair, unlike Watson, does not assign the date 1952 to the observations.
4. Keys, Ken (1984). The Hundredth Monkey. Camarillo: DeVorss & Co. ISBN 0-942024-01-X.
5. Whiten, Andrew; J. Goodall; W. C. McGrew; T. Nishida; V. Reynolds; Y. Sugiyama; C. E. G. Tutin; R. W. Wrangham; C. Boesch (1999). "Cultures in chimpanzees". Nature. 399 (6737): 682–685. doi:10.1038/21415. PMID 10385119.
6. Boesch, Christophe (2012). "31. Culture in primates. A - Culture as it Happens". In Jaan Valsiner. The Oxford Handbook of Culture and Psychology (PDF). OUP. p. 678. ISBN 9780195396430.
7. Trivedi, Bijal P. (February 6, 2004). ""Hot Tub Monkeys" Offer Eye on Nonhuman "Culture"". National Geographic Channel October 28, 2010/National Geographic.
8. b Galef, B. G. (1992). "The question of animal culture". Human Nature. 3 (2): 157–178. doi:10.1007/BF02692251.
9. Wikipedia.org

NOTES

"Skeptic Earth" – The Oroborus Effect

Following the "Great Global Ascension" to the next level of consciousness, the sceptics that could not believe that such a thing was/is possible, were left behind. That society now consists of 100% scepticism on all accounts, and laws are made to support the same. If someone states a fact, there is always someone else to take up arms against the fact, no matter how obvious the fact may be. To explore anything but scepticism is punishable by death; as death is the only absolute.

Since everything is based upon scepticism, there is no exploration into creation, as arguably so... creation does not exist. Those considering such action will be put to death. Even the creation of new arguments for the same old thing can be suggestive of creation. In turn, the punishment is the same.

Therefore, society can only digress to the lowest forms of information. Eventually, society disintegrates and the population collapses down to a primordial level, as that is the only state that cannot be challenged. They have learned that silence is the only defence. Over time, the evolution of a mute civilization is created with those few remaining.

NOTE:
Scepticism only exists from the structure of creation. When primordial man began to use fire, there was another one there that grunted, "You are going to get burned!" When there is no creation, there is nothing to be sceptic against.

Moral - Arrogance blinds those that consider themselves or their discipline perfect.

Intellectuals' Edict: - The Crucible Against Change

Scientists are quite often wrong. Often these imperfections are discovered well after the first discoveries are made. Thus we often live in the shadow of imperfection, because the hierarchy does not like to give up its position without a fight. This is most present in disciplines such as Archaeology, where history is date stamped. When an anomaly to that indexing is challenged by facts as something new arises, most times it is put down to forged results. If discoveries still challenge the system, then the system goes into denial.

"We create history by our observation, rather than history creating us."
— Stephen Hawking, The Grand Design

NOTES

Chapter 3
Photographic Memory

Photographic Memory - The Holy Grail of Brain Development

What the Photographic Memory is, or is not, has polarized the intellectual community to support or deny its existence. To rationalize the existence of the photographic memory is to first understand the **"eidetic memory"**.

In my daily efforts to teach people they have a fantastic force they can use for their own benefit, I tell them about the photographic memory - why you once had it, what happened to it, how you can gain it back, what it looks like to you, how to take advantage of it, and the interesting story behind why it is so controversial.

I have written many articles about the photographic memory in my blog at MindToMind.com. (Please type "photographic memory" into the search bar. You will find plenty.)

What is the Photographic Memory?

You were born with an "eidetic" memory. This is the memory that makes you the *infant genius information sponge* your parents remember. The eidetic memory processes information from all of your senses - touch, taste, smell, sight, hearing, and even input from additional sources, referred to as your sixth sense.

The eidetic memory is the one phenomenal possession you are born with that you use to learn the most difficult things to learn, such as language, social skills, and many more. It differentiates humans from all other life on the planet. Your eidetic memory is a NATURAL function of your brain. You never lose it. You will always have it available. You automatically use it, without you knowing it. (I will explain this point later.)

However, the term "photographic memory" is invented, made up, a fabrication, a falsehood, a lie, and some would have you believe it does not exist. The truth is downright bizarre.

THE TRUTH: When people began to discuss this in the complicated terms of psychology, the word "eidetic" was difficult to remember. It does not fit well 'on the tongue', and sounds worse if you mispronounce it. Joe Public needed a different word, that was easy to remember and easily understood. Thus the word "Photographic Memory" was born. Since most people learn visually (65%), it was the obvious word to use instead of eidetic.

Is it wrong to make up the word photographic memory just because eidetic is the type of word you would rather not have to say at all? Perhaps it was the wrong thing to do. Today, since the word "photographic memory" is made up, a misnomer, it is the basis for a polarized argument over the existence of the photographic memory.

On one side of the fence, there are people that happily say the photographic memory exists, as it is only another name for the eidetic memory. On the other side, the non-believers line up to denounce the photographic memory as something rather evil, to be stricken from all knowledge. With the level of malevolence against the word, it should tell you to look for an agenda. Why would they fear for the public to be aware the photographic memory is real? It is Natural. Why all the fuss?

The Photographic Memory is the same thing as the Eidetic Memory.

Now that I have disclosed the origin of the photographic memory, for convenience, I will continue to use it for better communication with the reader.

Photographic Memory and Global Consciousness

Global consciousness plays a big part in the concept of the photographic memory.

The photographic memory is treasured as an edge over the public by elitists. In higher private schools, their ideals support the photographic memory as a natural attribute for use in later life. While in public schooling, it has been systematically stripped out by the way reading is taught.

In public school, and even most private schools, to learn reading, you are told to forget and suppress your natural abilities, which up until that time served you so well. You learned everything so easily before. In this way, reading is taught in direct opposition with the NATURAL photographic memory. You are told to leave your childish ways behind. Most through guilt, persuasion, and systematic bullying and punishment, give in to their master's onslaught.

NOTE: The perceived reason for school is; You are to be taught and use a more effective better way to learn, right? TRUTH: Your learning ability goes down once you enter the formal education system (school).

(National Education Association Statistics)

The Photographic Memory - Hollywood Creates Impossible Expectations

Hollywood loves embellishing most things for shock value. The photographic memory is one of those things. The image portrayed of the Hollywood style photographic memory does not exist, nor serve most people wanting to regain access to their photographic memory. That particular level of photographic memory can be quite a burden.

At present, there are currently less than 100 people catalogued to have a full access photographic recall memory, or HSAM (Highly Superior Autobiographical Memory). Here is a list of issues typical with this type of photographic memory:

HSAM (Highly Superior Autobiographical Memory)

Many of these people have an enlarged region in the brain (often referred to as a medical condition) associated with the basal ganglia - the Caudate Nucleus, which resides close to the hippocampus (short term memory) in the limbic system.

Currently, since there are not many people available for testing, it is not clear whether the enlargement is the precursor or the product of the HSAM ability.

Some of the HSAM people became aware of the ability during puberty. Again, the information is ambiguous with regards as to when any changes or abnormalities occurred adjacent to when the condition is first noticed.

NOTE: The enlarged area of the brain with regards to HSAM is referred to negatively as a "medical condition". Other occurrences of enlargements to certain regions of the brain include athletes involved in 3-dimension or aerial gymnastics requiring they know where they are in 3-dimensional space. This is referred to as being **"gifted"**, NOT a medical condition.

Another common marker is the occurrence of OCD (Obsessive Compulsive Disorder). Some brain specialists suspect the caudate nucleus may play a role in the development of obsessive compulsive disorder. The OCD tends to appear as orderly placement, often in the person's wardrobe as to how their clothes are "obsessively orderly" (every mother's dream...). These OCD traits would likely be unrecognizable when the person is autistic since caregivers would likely manage their daily routine.

The **caudate nucleus** plays a significant role in how the brain learns, storing and processing of memories, and uses information from past experiences to influence future actions and decisions, and impacts development and use of language.

Professor James McGaugh, University of California, Irvine, the primary researcher in HSAM (Highly Superior Autobiographical Memory), during a 60-minute interview, revealed that he has observed an effect as to how these people correlate the information with a computer-like 'tabulating effect' as the data is shuffled into place. This is the same effect many Brain Management clients experience as a result of using Mental Photography.

HSAM (Highly Superior Autobiographical Memory) References...

McGaugh, J.L. Making lasting memories: Remembering the significant. Proceedings, National Academy of Sciences, USA, 110 (2), 2013, 10401-10407.

McGaugh, J.L. and Leport, A. Highly superior autobiographical memory. Scientific American, February 2014, 40-45.

Another expression of excessive involvement of photographic memory includes...

> Autistic Savants (Idiot Savants) - These people are often isolated from normal interaction that can be stressful. They usually have minders or caregivers that make their decisions for

them. Change in routine can be catastrophic. Most have little to no volume control over their memories.

Typical issues include: cannot reduce the volume, no screening before viewing, no conscious filter system. A single "wrong" word can trigger a series of overwhelming memories that they don't want to have. This becomes a serious disability.

The average person has 5 bad events to 1 good event every day. Your conscious filtering system screens these out, so you only ponder or remember the memories you choose. Usually, you are not forced to relive bad memories over and over again.

For this <u>full-on recall photographic memory experience</u>, the results can be agoraphobia and anthropophobia. These people are often burdened with low self esteem, negativity, suicidal thoughts, and often cared for in facilities. Treatments may include drugs to suppress the ongoing anxieties and depression. Panic attacks are common.

The good thing - if you are NOT burdened with this recall ability totally switched on without any screening in place, you can use your photographic memory safely. Your mind will automatically have the conscious level screening already in place to prevent the potential flood of out of control memories.

What you should expect as you begin to take control of your photographic memory:

> Since you may not have been accessing your photographic memory directly for a number of years, reopening this door may seem futile at first. I provide various methods to help you with opening the door and growing the pathways, opening the **"Superhighway"** the photographic memory uses for high

volume information flow. With consistent effort, our clients begin to experience more and more. Some clients say it feels like they are guessing at first. When the answers just keep coming, the idea of guessing is discarded.

Your memory will get better.

Your decision making process will be much easier and clearer than before.

Many other seemingly unrelated events will happen in your life as the exercises I provide strengthen your brain overall. Your photographic memory is your gateway to limitless ability.

Your conscious mind is not familiar with how these things are happening. The conscious mind cannot assimilate information as the subconscious can. Thus, the conscious mind goes into denial and will give you feedback that the photographic memory isn't working for you. Brain Management has a number of ways that "show" your conscious mind you are having real results. Your conscious mind will continue to resist for a long time. Through consistent use, the conscious mind will accept it.

Ultimately, you will have more knowledge and wisdom than you ever thought possible. It will take your time and perseverance to get there. **That is what it takes to gain back access to something you already have, which was stolen away from you when you were most vulnerable - as a child. The re-enabling process goes against the conditioning you received from others denouncing the existence of your photographic memory.**

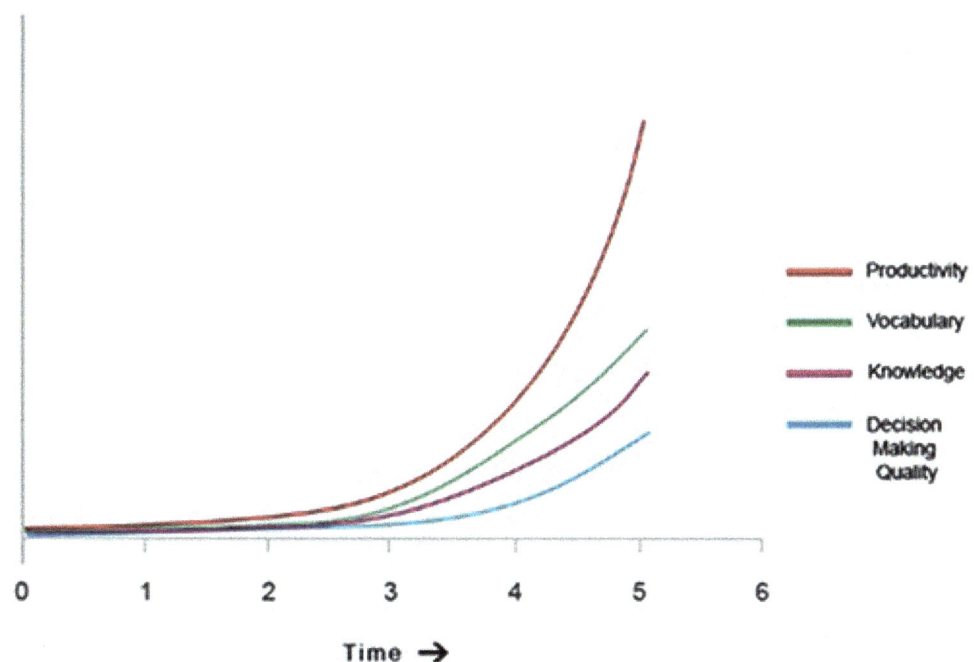

Growth From Using Photographic Memory

Why do most people abandon their photographic memory?

Global consciousness plays a big part in how most people think about reading, which is a conscious level activity, and the photographic memory, which is subconscious. This impacts your belief that the photographic memory exists. To regain access to your photographic memory, you must first believe that your photographic memory resides within you. You would change this within your individual consciousness using specific methods and personal programming to support your results.

Your photographic memory is exercised and used every day.

Earlier I mentioned I would tell you how your photographic memory is already being used without your knowing...

Subliminal advertising and other subliminal manipulations are using your photographic memory to program your brain to react in ways that are not necessarily in your best interests. (The subliminal programs you were exposed to as children are still there in your subconscious; still programming you to this day. Over time and exposure, you may have billions of these old outdated, unknown, and unneeded programs. They cause problems with your decision making process. I have created specific steps to rid my clients of these menacing programs.) Since the subliminal programs and subliminal advertising use the same pathway as your photographic memory to install their programs into your mind, then your photographic memory is healthy and well-oiled; and ready for you to step in and take charge of it.

Your photographic memory is the same as the eidetic memory you were born with, it is a **completely natural brain function** for you to take control of, for your own benefit. Once you do this, it will empower you like nothing else.

The global consciousness has provided you a false path to follow that does not include you having access to, nor using, your natural photographic memory. Only by using your will-power and steadfast resolve will you be able to win this consciousness battle. The results you achieve by using your photographic memory will enable you to change your belief, and make it a part of your individual consciousness and your personal holographic universe.

Your photographic memory is your legacy of being human.

Summary: You may be wondering why the photographic memory is such an important topic regarding consciousness. Exercising your photographic memory exercises your brain to be stronger and more resilient. It opens your perspective to higher realities, builds memory, and makes everything you do easier. Mental Photography, using your photographic memory, is "applied Quantum Physics"; viewing information as thought patterns, energy, and frequency – at light speed.

NOTES

Chapter 4
Global Consciousness Universal Consciousness

Differences between Global Consciousness and Universal Consciousness

In a nutshell; while the global consciousness is the driving force that compels you to follow certain ideals and beliefs that are present on the planet at this time, the Universal Consciousness brings things into being that have not manifested into this reality yet. This is sometimes referred to as the birthplace of invention. Therefore, universal consciousness mostly works with the perceived future and what that holds in store for us. While all parts of our consciousness hold access to this magnificent source of information, it is the universal consciousness that holds most sway over what we access and when.

Even though all forms of consciousness are intrinsically connected and have relationships to each other, it is our own limited perspective and desire to place valuations upon each as to how we are connected to each of them. In itself it is the grand illusion, as we are born of a consciousness which we then interact with from that point forward forever into infinity. This in turn brings forward the two questions, **"Are we ever born?"**, and **"Do we ever die?"** That would suggest a Shiva moment - creation from destruction, annihilation brings rebirth, in the same moment.

Sudden Insight - Invention

The Law of Attraction simply works. You can attract new things never before known. Suddenly you have an idea or thought come to you that you never had before. Nobody is immune to the Law of Attraction. Some of these ideas can be inventions that have fallen into your lap - to be invented at this particular moment in time. It happens because the world is ready for it to happen. Why does it happen this way? Why does anything happen at all? It is marvellous how the universe "provides".

If you do not have the means to create, manage, distribute, and market the invention, fear not. When it landed in your lap, it also landed in the lap of millions of other receptive people. Someone amongst all those that received the idea will have the means to put it on the shelf, where you can admire the "thing" you were destined to invent but didn't.

This is also referred to as universal knowledge. There is an infinite amount of data, information, creations, inventions, and things your mind cannot fathom. You may have heard, "All knowledge is rediscovered." Universal knowledge is available for you to tap into at any time. It is an infinite and inexhaustible resource.

In many ways, universal consciousness is much easier to utilise than global consciousness as global consciousness tends to be oppressive in its nature. Universal consciousness is what provides the rewards from using the Law of Attraction. By making changes within your beliefs to allow completely new and unforseen things to take place, you are accepting that universal consciousness provides to you. That in turn is felt in your individual consciousness by way of manifesting those things to magically appear in your life.

Chapter 5
Departure into the Abyss As Heaven Unfolds

Think of this...

Every movie, television show, book, unusual forms of information, and entertainment; especially science fiction and fantasy, depicts a single moment, a snapshot of another reality, existing as an entirely different dimension. What if they already exist? Perhaps we are reading the "Cosmic Newspaper"?

Every decision you make has two or more outcomes. In this dimension, you make one of the choices. In another dimension, a different choice is made. Each choice you make has its own path, leading to a myriad of other decisions. The result of each decision made becomes a new 'You', in a new dimension; a new universe. Now, multiply that infinite number by the other almost 8 billion people on this planet having similar experiences.
The number of worlds is infinite.

Some information provided in the next section of this book can only be considered speculative, as there is no public proof of the events in question.

Multiverse

The multiverse is a hypothetical group of multiple universes including the universe in which humans live. Together, these universes comprise everything that exists: the entirety of space, time, matter, energy, the physical laws and the constants that describe them. [It is considered 'hypothetical' because global consciousness has not provided clear proof of its existence.] - **Wikipedia**

"And since Space is divisible in infinitum, and Matter is not necessarily in all places, it may be also allow'd that God is able to create Particles of Matter of several Sizes and Figures, and in several Proportions to Space, and perhaps of different Densities and Forces, and thereby to vary the Laws of Nature, and make Worlds of several sorts in several Parts of the Universe. At least, I see nothing of Contradiction in all this."
- **Sir Isaac Newton**, From his book "Optics", 1704

Quantum Physicists have discovered other dimensions than the three dimensions (x, y, z) we actively take part in, in a physical way. However, that does not mean that we do not participate with other dimensions in non-physical ways. Though the nature of the Universe being infinite; once that small gap is opened, there are an infinite number of ways to view and access the other dimensions. If science already has the way to visit these other realms, they are keeping it quite secret.

The question to consider at this time is, "Why does it seem that discoveries and inventions are created in a timely sequence, and not some erratic and random event, such as inventing something we would not even know what it would be used for in the next 100 years?"

Consider this...

*"That multiverse idea is not a notion invented to account for the miracle of fine-tuning. It is a consequence of the no-boundary condition as well as many other theories of modern cosmology. But if it is true, then the strong anthropic principle (The anthropic principle is a philosophical consideration that observations of **the universe must be compatible with the conscious and sapient life that observes it.**) can be considered effectively equivalent to the weak one, putting the fine-tunings of physical law on the same footing as the environmental factors, for it means that our cosmic habitat—now the entire observable universe—is only one of many, just as our solar system is one of many.*

That means that in the same way that the environmental coincidences of our solar system were rendered unremarkable by the realization that billions of such systems exist, the fine-tunings in the laws of nature can be explained by the existence of multiple universes."
- Stephen Hawking

It has been said that some things, impossible things, instantaneously manifest into our reality, to instantly pop out of existence, as it is not compatible with the "conscious and sapient life that observes it". Since the global consciousness dictates that the masses do not yet possess the ability to think or believe in these fantastic ways, then finding all of the answers may just be a little out of reach until the masses begin to think in these directions. However the quantum scientist can reveal to the smaller group that the evidence exists. This will not impact the global consciousness until the critical number is met.

NOTES

Chapter 6
Exit The Ordinary

Departure to Cryptozoology and Forbidden Archaeology in this dimension

Consider how we look at "Cryptozoology". Most people would be sceptical about the existence of many things outside of the ordinary knowledge base, such as mythological creatures - Himalayan Yeti, North American Big Foot, Andean Roc, and the Loch Ness Monster to name a few. They tend to be located in very remote areas which makes confirmation of their existence difficult.

The lore and legends of giants is still part of the culture of tribes and religions around the world. Archaeology continues to make finds, just to have them denounced as hoaxes, officials removing bones and evidence to be hidden or destroyed; or cover-ups by groups that believe the human race should not know of these beings' existence, as it goes against the current global agendas. In the past, publications such as "Forbidden Archaeology" were banned from schools and universities for presenting empirical evidence that is outside of the accepted time-line and data taught. Control of information further structures the inhibition of thought within the Global Consciousness.

Multiverse Threatens Stability of Global Consciousness

Using the Multiverse example, the Earth would have an infinite amount of overlays or layers we just cannot see. They are out of synch with our own. The solutions to this world's greatest problems could be "within reach", if we only knew how to travel to, or access, the other realms safely.

These other dimensions are mentioned in ancient texts and studies. There are reportedly E Adepts and Masters that can easily travel between these layers. It is said they would 'slip away' into an alternative dimension, only to appear somewhere else in this world in the next moment. This conditioning would take great memory, as this type of travel has dangers associated with it. Once the Adept would slip into the other dimension, he would then mentally focus on a detailed mental picture of where he would want to wind up before slipping back into this world.

Imagine how it would be if you were that Master. You could travel without a Passport or Visa. (I guess someone would have something to say about that...) Imagine if you chose to go to Paris, and the reference you have is a picture of the Eiffel Tower. What if that picture was taken at 30 feet off the ground. You might be surprised when you rematerialise 30 feet off of the ground. That would be quite a surprise! That is just one reason why this type of travel can be dangerous.

What if you picked the wrong dimension to step off into to begin your travel? Time could be flowing at a very different rate than you are accustomed to. Your aging process could be altered, or you could be away for many years, and it only feels like an instant to you. Remember, time is only an illusion. For another dimension, its' relative rate of time would be according to that dimension.

When we discuss how we should observe, travel to, or enter into other dimensions, there are many interpretations and explanations, both by adepts and believers, and quantum scientists that seek to understand the subtleties that only Ethereal Adepts can explain.

Imagine This, to Infinity and Beyond...

Think of 1000 duplicates of Earth. This number is actually meant to be infinite, but for this exercise we will use 1000.

Some of the Earths can be almost an exact duplicate of our own. Some could be radically different. Here are a few differences you may experience:

>Perhaps the dinosaurs never went extinct and are the dominant life form.
>
>Perhaps humans only exist on a few of the Earths.
>
>Perhaps plants or Insects are the dominant life forms with no mammals.
>
>Perhaps the time rate is very fast or very slow.
>
>Perhaps the Earth is only a charred ball floating through space, the results of war or other cataclysmic disaster.
>
>Perhaps the Earth has been demolished, and only fragments float through space. Thus, there would be no atmosphere or air to breathe.
>
>Perhaps it has the surface of the moon with no atmosphere.
>
>Perhaps it is inhabited by aliens
>
>Perhaps magical creatures and dragons populate the planet.

The types of potential differences are endless.

NOTES

Draconis Invertis - Dragons vs. Dinosaurs

Have you ever given thought as to how many cultures have myths and legends about dragons? Sure, everyone has been told about a 'Wiseman' who goes on a journey. On the journey, he stumbles onto a skeleton of a prehistoric dinosaur, and proclaims to all that will listen that he has discovered a 'dragon'. Sure, that may be part of the story. Could there be a different story?

What if that same Mage is travelling through the dimensions, and visits a dimension where actual live dragons inhabit that particular dimension? More to the point, the dragons would be real, living, and breathing, and perhaps even belching fire. Wouldn't it be amazing if you could visit a place like that. You may not last very long. You would probably make a tasty snack to the dragons living there.

The legends about dragons are a global phenomenon. Most cultures would not consider them deities, although they are supposed to have magical and spiritual powers. Some dragons fly by magic, and have no wings. Other dragons fly with wings. While other dragons swim underwater. They may be serpentine, and others tend to be more like a flying lizard or snake-like, no matter what the size. Their appearance often ushers in omens. At other times, they seemingly just want to eat people (Apparently, their choice food is humans - often barbequed.)

When looking at the universe and multiverse and all the different contemplations that result in something with infinite possibility, you are bound to stumble onto such themes. Even the movies that have been created over the past 50 years or so have been indoctrinating everyone into considering the existence of other worlds. Perhaps those worlds are not far away after all. Perhaps they are just underfoot, just a slight turn to the left...

This is the implied magic of the chaotic star stuff that the quantum physicists speak of. However, there does seem to be a point of real interest in magnetics. Magnetism is an inexhaustible form of everlasting energy that flows throughout the universe. As the basis of how motors and generators function, it is a mystery. Magnetics are used in everything from the mundane to fusion reactors and more. Most of what we know about magnetism comes from observing the effect it has on other things.

NOTES

Chapter 7
Repercussions

Boomerang Effect - Life Threatening Repercussions

Implications of Psychological Instability - Diagnostics Applied to Humans as a Result of Inadvertent Interaction with Multiple Dimensions, Alternative Realities, and Life Forms Not Endemic to this Dimension, can lead to a False Diagnosis of Psychosis, Forced Medication, and Institutionalised Imprisonment.

When a person's observations on various witnessed events are not in accordance with the mean-average, humanity has taken on the authoritarian role of subjugator and ajudicator of witnesses or participants who have been presented with other worldly happenings. There seems to be a pervasive attitude to stamp out anything that does not follow the normal line of thinking. There is no room for amorphous, ambiguous, nebulous, or fractured thought processes; as they show symptoms of instability.

In this way, the partiality of psychiatric professionals is often one-sided to facilitate a profession that is proven to have more problems than the "patients" they are treating. Licensing limits the quality of the treatments that can be administered only to the limit covered by the professional's licence. Unfortunately, one of the treatments that seems to withstand that limitation is the dosing of psychotropic drugs. Since the 1950s when first invented, there has been an alarming rise in the number of people under this type of treatment.

Critical information of psychotropic drug usage:
- Other institutions, such as **Harvard Medical** and **Psychology Today** have raised the alarm as psychotropic drugs are prescribed too frequently, and often without proper observation of the patient.
- The highest group of people taking antidepressants - 1 in 4 women in their 40s and 50s.

- In 2016, *Live Science* reported; 1 in 6 Americans are on psychotropic drugs

Psychiatric professionals often hide behind officialised and formalised systems of testing to vindicate subjugation of normal, usually frightened, people. Intimidation is commonly used to push them to a fight or flight response, further justifying the need to immediately administer medication.

Most psychological tests are geared to find the person being tested to be unstable, even when the person is completely sane and normal. *(The justification for the weight of the test to be against the person, is the assumption the person would not undergo testing unless they are demonstrating significant erratic behavior patterns outside of what is an opinion of normal. Therefore, these tests are meant to verify what the professionals "already know", and that only unstable people are the people to be tested. The tests are NOT to prove sanity.)* When the person being scrutinized answers honestly, they would likely be assessed as unstable, insane, or mentally ill.

Once the person is assessed as mentally ill, whether true or not, the person is usually medicated "for their own good". If the person refuses medication, some institutions have the legal right to restrain and forcibly administer medication. The system has a way of self-perpetuating its own patients based on such reproachful methods.

Further life-long harm is done to the person's self-esteem and confidence. They may lose their employment, or be refused employment, prevented from accessing life insurance or have it taken away from them, as this would show up on their medical record for the rest of their life. Even Credit Cards and loan financers have access to these records; and they do not need to provide any reason why they are turning a person down. That very same person begins to feel the world is against them, even when the event that caused it all has been left far behind in the past. Many of them begin to feel they are just the terrible person the system claims they are which can perpetuate self harm.

Here is a partial list of repercussions that many people are already experiencing. Most will continue to experience it for the rest of their life, and be completely unaware as to the reason why. Once medical records are documented with such issues, the evidence is high that the following can take place:

- Driver's License suspended
- Visa revoked
- Travel restricted
- Travel prohibited on airplanes
- Prohibited from going into certain places, like government buildings
- Life Insurance revoked or denied
- Loss of job
- Unhireable
- Listed as "subversive", and/or placed on "Watch Lists"
- Heredity mention into children's medical history can affect your children the same way.
- ...many other things too

It has been suggested that more than 95% of all encounters are NOT reported out of fear of these types of actions happening.

IMPORTANT NOTE: I first wanted to bring this important information to your attention so you will not dismiss the gravity of ongoing manipulations and agendas being used against ordinary people. **There are a good percentage of psychiatric and psychological professionals doing the "good work".** Optimistically, I believe more than 50% have not been led down the Dark Side of acting without high integrity. Going down that path is a great temptation, and often it is a consequence of the organization they are working for, simply by adhering to treatment policies. The implications weigh heavily on personal consciousness and global consciousness, and everyone's right to better themselves and be more productive. My message is, "Be cautious if you find you are in jeopardy."

Magnetism - Unlimited Power Source

Magnetism is one of the great mysteries of life. Whether it be huge magnetic fields or an insignificant magnet held in your hand; Though the strength is very different, the lines of magnetic force extend out into space and go on forever. It perplexes scientists, as it is an everlasting source of power.

Our world exists on magnetism and the things it affects. Ancient knowledge about magnetism is just as valid today. Basic and simple, yet the effects can be widely varied in nature. This energy can result in various localised anomalies.

Ley Lines...

Ley lines are magnetic lines of force that run all over the Earth. It is the Earth's magnetic grid. As the molten (iron) core of the Earth rotates, it causes magnetic fields to be created, like a massive generator. They go through the Earth, then emanate out into space. These lines of force have a direct effect on gravitation and space-time. Likewise, they are connected with consciousness; at all levels.

Ley lines are most easily detectible by dowsing. With dowsing, our mind's energy field connects with the energy field of the Earth. We find that ley lines have been used since the beginning of building structures of significance (monoliths), and then into more sophisticated structures, like churches. In the natural world, if a tree is growing near a disharmonious ley line, it will bend out of the way. This action forms what appears to be a natural path through the trees.

Ancient Wisdom Carried Over for Modern Applications

Ancient monoliths and megaliths are often set in relation to the natural ley lines - Stonehenge being one of many. The pyramids are built in alignment with ley lines. This technology of using these energy points for 'talking with God' was adapted for the geographical placement of medieval churches and cathedrals in the Middle Ages. Many churches intersected with ley lines. One of the most famous ley lines in Britain is the St. Michael's Ley. It has prehistoric sites, many churches, and other significant sites located on it. Many of them are named St Michael and St. George, both are "dragon slaying" saints.

The typified footprint for a church or cathedral built in the Middle Ages is in the shape of a cross. If possible, the altar would be at the East end, or sometimes in the middle where the structure forms an X in the middle. Optimally, the cross footprint would be placed over two ley lines at 90 degrees to each other. The intersection of the two lines would be the strategic position for the altar. As ley lines would move a little over time, the altar needed to be moved to maintain its critical position. Thus, some old churches show signs where the floor stones had been cut and replaced to accommodate the movement of the altar. If the spire were placed over this point, it would act as an upshoot for the vortex created at the intersection of the ley lines. It would then act to send the prayers of the congregation to God.

The Magnetosphere, like the Ionosphere, is ~500 miles above the Earth's surface. As the Earth rotates, it causes a differential between the surface of the Earth and the magnetosphere. This difference creates a potential from where electricity can be drawn. This is the same "free energy" that Nicola Tesla was working with and promoting as a benefit for all people to access and use "wirelessly".

Ley lines often intersect with other ley lines. The result is a vortex. The closer the intersection is to 90 degrees, the greater the amount of energy can go through it, relative to the strength of the two ley lines. At these intersections, upshoots and downshoots are created. Upshoots send energy up to the magnetosphere and downshoots direct energy down from the magnetosphere. Both of these can be regulated by using an Obelisk. The material the obelisk is made from is significant to the direction of energy flow.

Right and Wrong Ways to Apply Obelisks

Care should be taken when placing an obelisk. An example of a correct placement of an obelisk as a downshoot would be the Washington Monument in Washington, D.C. This obelisk will pull energy into the city from the Heavens. An example of a wrong place to place an obelisk is a graveyard or cemetery. In that case, the energy coming down through the obelisk would give energy to the dead.

Washington Monument and the Lincoln Memorial Reflection Pool . Image credit: US Government

Above are the Washington Monument and the Lincoln Memorial Reflection Pool. The strategic arrangement of these two monuments has specific energetic significance. As with regards to Egyptology and the teachings of the Rosicrucian Order and Freemasonry, - having the mirror image of the obelisk doubles its power. "As above, so below."

Other structures that change or direct the magnetics of ley lines include pyramids and geodesic domes. Portals to other dimensions are created when three lines cross in close proximity to each other. The closer the angles get to 90/45/45 degrees, the more likely a portal can be formed. Since each ley line has its own energy and frequency, it may take the correct combination for the portal to open.

You may be wondering what all these natural anomalies and events regarding naturally occurring magnetics has to do with consciousness or the multiverse? Ancient records within the memories and pictograms from ancient cultures indicate this knowledge is nothing new. Ancient peoples were more in tune with their natural environment, and reacted to it accordingly. This led to esoteric and magical discoveries that Shamen and Wise Men could use to do unusual things.

The uses of subtle energies are very effective in the natural world. You just must know the right thing to do at the right time.

Good Scientists Never let Subtleties get in the Way of Progress.

When X-Rays were first invented, it was highly likely the patient would die from radiation poisoning after having a series of x-rays. Rather counterproductive. Today, you can have many x-rays taken, even with layers, without needing to feel that you are in any serious danger of exceeding your limit. Over time, we found ways to turn down the dose, and refine the amount of energy and frequency to 'just enough' to do the job. Since most of what is known about other dimensions is mostly legend, the delicate parameters of exploring these areas in a scientific way is unknown.

Worse yet, is if there is military involvement. With military might, they have the propensity to want to not only blow the doors open, but blow up the building at the same time, when only a little fine tuning is all that is needed. These are now referred to as "Smart Bombs".

The battle cry of many past Generals... **"A good bomb is only a good bomb when it is blown up."** Brute force assault on translocating into an alternative dimension can have unknown consequences. Whereas, since a person's mind writes and rewrites consciousness daily, it is the key to controlling and tuning subtle energies. This is also what the Ethereal Adepts use to travel into those realms.

The "Philadelphia Experiment" - Lesson NOT Learned...

USS Eldridge. Photo credit: US Government

A military experiment in 1943, during WW II, working with high energy magnetics to "shift" an entire ship, the USS Eldridge, into another dimension and bend light as a means to hide the ship, or make it invisible, is a good example how unexpected results can go very bad. Additionally the USS Eldridge was teleported to Norfolk, VA and back to the Philadelphia Shipyard. This was referred to as **"The Philadelphia Experiment"**. The experiment actually did succeed. But it killed most of the sailors on board. "There is infinitely more space between sub-molecular particles than the particles take up." Therefore, you can pass one solid object right through another and neither will touch the other - provided they are out of phase with each other.

In this case, when the ship rematerialised, there were various parts of the sailors bodies that were embedded and stuck halfway through a wall or a thick steel deck. Yes, they were dead or dying. Reports of sailors spontaneously catching fire, disappearing, or insane from the scrambling of their molecules were common. Some sailors' bodies were never recovered. The whole event was hushed and the tests were halted (at that time). Further experiments were carried out later. Witnesses came forward and made claims that the testing has never stopped. The entire event was clouded in government secrecy and cover-up.

The Philadelphia Experiment incident was always denied by the government.. Since it was wartime, the sailors that died were said to have been "lost at sea". Their families were never told the truth.

NOTES

Reports regarding the Large Hadron Collider at CERN...

There have been many observations made around the surrounding area and in the atmosphere above the LHC. Anomalies include UFOs, flying spheres, documentation of strange lights and designs in the sky directly above LHC, and more. Some researchers allege the LHC has been used for creating 2-way portals between dimensions, and this work has been ongoing for quite some time. At the same time, there are extreme warnings issued from other researchers about the dangers of doing this work. Weapons and containment may not be enough to stop *them* from coming through the portal or "getting out". Ohhh, the arrogance.

"Success in creating AI would be the biggest event in human history. Unfortunately, it might also be the last, unless we learn how to avoid the risks." – Stephen Hawking

Trust Your Government to Protect You, ... From the Truth?

"History is Doomed to repeat itself". The first reason is history is always altered in some way, and you never get the full story. The second reason is people forget. People do not exercise their memory; therefore, they forget what has happened before. Governments and the military anticipate that most people will forget the details of any event. They are watchful of people who have a functioning photographic memory, as they are considered a threat to the agenda(s). Perhaps this is also the reason why governments have staged such an elaborate ruse to force people away from using their natural photographic memory and enslave them with ineffective reading.

Localized Effects of Magnetic Fields, Ley Lines, and Magnetic Anomalies...

Observations of instabilities in regions of naturally high levels of magnetics and/or high numbers of Ley Lines. WARNING: The act of observing and reporting such events is considered psychologically inappropriate, and the observer may be subject to psychological evaluation in many countries. Since many people would be fearful of reporting such events, it leads us to consider just how many events go unreported.

Such events may be referred to as legend, lore, flights of fancy, intoxication, or a drugged stupor. However, there are an ever-increasing number of reports of events that do not have a logical explanation.. Many are consistently experienced at dusk, or just after the sun has set, and in areas of naturally occurring high magnetic energy.

NOTES

Ley Lines, Vortexes, 3-D Portals (x, y, z), and 4-D Portals (x, y, z, t)...

Ley Lines are the magnetic grid of the Earth. They run all over the Earth. Each line has its own signature. It is a waveform. So, it has an amplitude - the height of the top to the bottom of the wave, the frequency - the time it takes for the wave to repeat, and the energy or power of the wave. The frequency of the wave may be short, or it may be long. Some wave frequencies can be measured in days. Since the ley lines go in all directions, they often intersect other ley lines. This junction is referred to as a vortex - a point where the magnetics undergo a change due to the interaction of the ley lines.

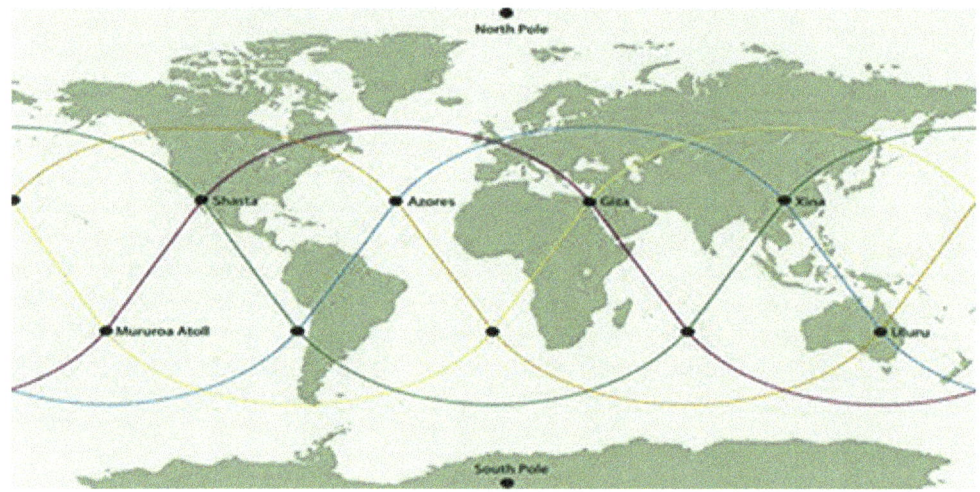

Earth's major ley line grid. Image by Dr Shannon Panzo

The map above shows Earth's major ley line grid. Please notice the similarities between Ley Line map and the 3-phase Power map below. Is this one of the relationships that Nicola Tesla understood on a global scale for his production of free energy?

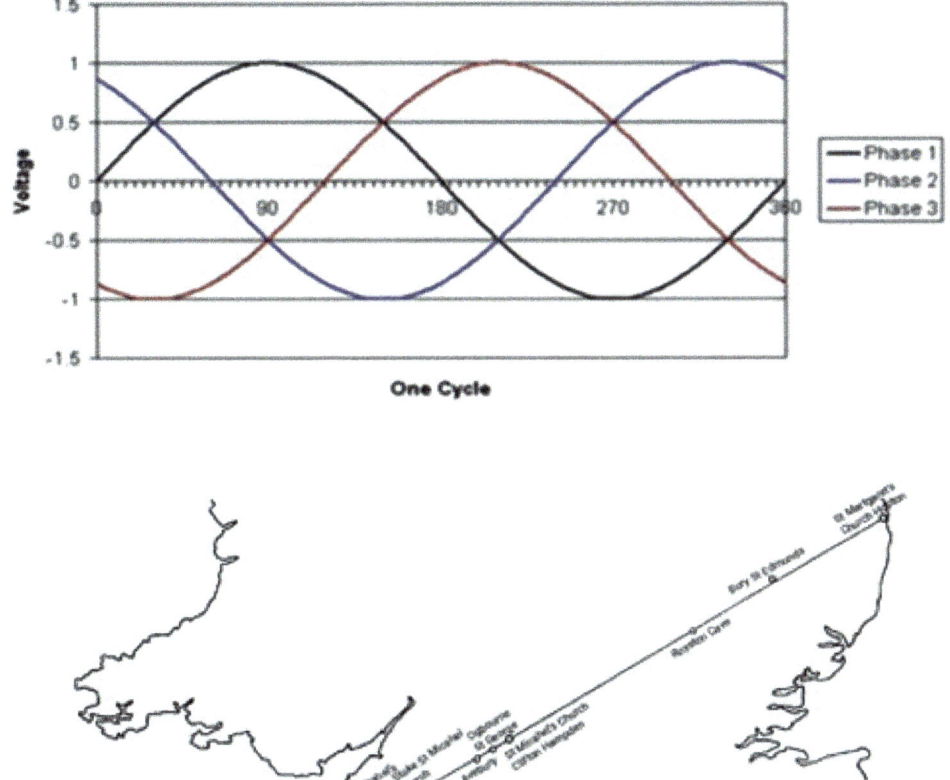

The Saint Michaels Ley Line. Diagram by Dr Shannon Panzo

The diagram above shows the strategic placement of many churches and ancient monolithic structures upon the Saint Michael's Ley Line that runs through the United Kingdom. The church names refer to Saint Michael and Saint George, both of whom are noted "dragon killers".

The chance that 1 ley line will be in tune, or balanced, with an intersecting ley line is seldom. Since the corresponding junctions are between two dissimilar ley lines, the harmonics will change as the intersecting energy characteristics change. Likewise the characteristics of the natural vortex will change likewise. The angle of approach of the two ley lines also makes a difference as to how much energy will be created at the vortex. As the angle gets closer to 90°, it makes the vortex stronger.

NOTES

Doorways and Portals...

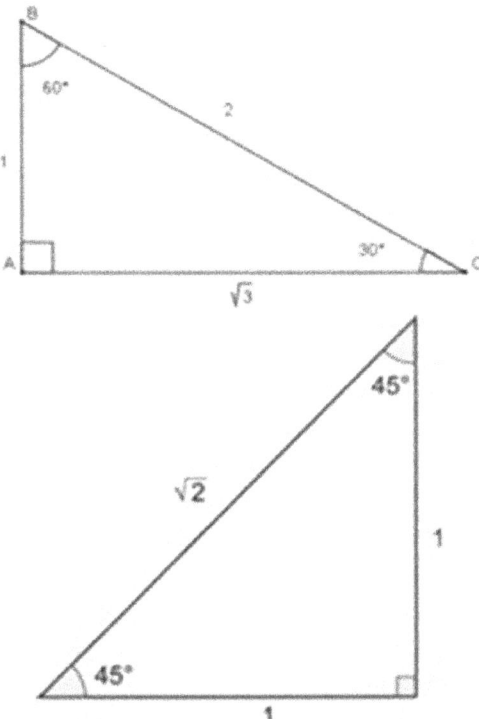

Above, the two triangles show the different intersections of Ley Lines make to create the optimum portal construction Given that all ley Lines shown in this representation are relatively equal in value, the 45°/45°/90° portal will be more effective and have more energy than the 30°/60°/90° portal.

When three or more ley lines converge within a few feet of each other, a 3-Dimensional portal or doorway into other dimensions can be created. The existing parameters of the ley lines and their interactions determine the stability of the portal, and which dimensions it can access. Access to open the portal is created by the thought power of your mind; your consciousness. Your mind is easily powerful enough to influence this. It is recommended that an Ethereal Adept would only traverse a stable portal, because it is easier to find the way back.

Other portals can have additional variances of the energy and frequency of converging ley lines creating 4-Dimensional doorways, where time (t) is the fourth dimension. This adds an additional risk to the traveler as time can be moving at different rates, even opposite or backwards time; whereas a person would emerge younger than before they stepped through the portal. Another possible outcome could be this dimension has progressed by 100 or 1000 years when the person steps back into this dimension. It is suggested that some of the portals around the Bermuda Triangle work this way.

These interdimensional portals can also allow entities from other realms into this dimension. So, if the portal is located in your living room, you may have more to talk about than the nightly news. If you have one located in a sensitive area, then the option of sealing it off can be employed, so you don't have unexpected visitors.

Areas with high levels of naturally occurring magnetism are often hotbeds for extraterrestrial and interdimensional activity. Care must be taken to avoid blocking or changing the ley lines in these areas. This can upset the balance and cause considerable unanticipated results. Tread lightly.

Why does interdimensional activity concentrate in magnetically charged areas?

Consider radio waves and the Ionosphere ... During the day, the various energy coming from the Sun causes disturbance throughout the Ionosphere. This means that radio waves can easily escape out into space. HAM Radio Operators have long known how to bounce radio waves off of the Ionosphere to communicate with other operators on the other side of the Earth; but it can only be done after the Sun sets. Once the Sun sets, the Ionosphere settles down and provides a mirror-like surface for the radio waves to be bounced off.

Consider the fabric of space and time to be resistant to intrusion from other dimensions. Added to this, the Sun's energy further agitates the "veil" and makes it impenetrable - <u>during the day</u>. Once the Sun sets and dusk occurs, the Sun's agitating energy is removed. The local magnetic energy destabilises what makes up the veil. The veil becomes thin. Interdimensional beings can easily move between the planes. Their consciousness does not register any difference between their dimension and our own, so when the fabric between dimensions warps and becomes weak, they can just walk across. Transdimensional beings do not need a portal to travel between dimensions.

These entities may or may not be human-like. Most tend to be invisible, as they are typically shifted from the frequency we operate at. They have different rules of engagement. Their ways may be quite unstable to what you are accustomed to. Interaction is easier if you consider that you are the interloper. It is a safer position, as their rules of engagement may place you in harm's way. The more aggressive types tend to follow you with their eyes; raising the hackles on your neck, like burning holes into your back. They are "observing" and watching you. You may not be able to see them, but you can certainly feel them. Occasionally, you may catch a glimpse out of the corner of your eye. They are ancient. Some encounters may be dangerous and put your life at risk. If you find you are coming in contact with them, do your best to present yourself as friendly. You may not be given a second chance.

Use Your Senses to Detect Co-Habitation

Another observation worth mentioning... You may be walking along in an uninhabited area at dusk. Your mind begins to register things that seem just out of reach. (Close your eyes to elevate your other senses.) You may hear sounds of people talking, but it is garbled. You may sense the smells of cooking, but there is nothing around that would give off those odors. Or, you may smell offensive odors, or odors that are indescribable, as these may be from non-human types. You may feel like you are walking through an occupied village with activity going on around you, but just outside of your direct awareness. Often times they will be aware of your presence, just ignoring you.

No Good Deed (Honesty) Goes Unpunished...

Depending on where you live and the circumstances you encountered, it may be Illegal to have contact with Extraterrestrials, Interdimensional Beings, Transdimensional Beings, and life forms not endemic to this dimension. Even travel into other dimensions may be prohibited. **Irony** – Most governments will deny the existence of such things, but they still make laws against such things from happening.

Describing these types of interactions to others may be seen as symptoms of psychosis. You should be careful who you tell. Imagine how many people having real contact with other dimensions and the inhabitants or transdimensionals are institutionalized, drugged, or have committed suicide, because they did not know how to handle interactions with alternative realities. They had not been indoctrinated with thinking outside the box. Their consciousness is stretched to the limit. Sometimes it breaks.

If you happen to find yourself being interviewed by psychologists or psychiatrists regarding such events, the first thing you must remember is **psychiatric tests are weighed against the person being tested**. These are tests to determine the level or degree of your mental illness. They are NOT to determine if you are sane. It is automatically assumed that for you to be tested at all, that you are mentally unstable. If you decline to take the tests, it is likely that you will be forcefully medicated, and possibly institutionalized.

Repercussions are life-long. Once your medical records are documented with such, evidence has shown many control mechanisms can be further used against you that will blockade most normal things you want to do in your life; even to the point of having a job or owning a car.

It has been suggested that more than 95% of all encounters are NOT reported for fear of repercussions.

Many unusual things can happen when the veil between worlds becomes thin.

Chapter 8
Confusione Ascensionem

(Ascension Confusion)

I recommend for every person to study what other great people have remarked about ascension, and come to their own understanding of what it represents to you. In other words, there is not one right answer. It is for you to figure out how it best relates to you.

Ascension

You cannot write a book about Consciousness without the topic of Ascension rising up like a wave, and cresting in front of you.

Ascension is an essential inclusion on any talk of Consciousness. Ascension is the ultimate prize and the ultimate escape at the same time. Depending which version you subscribe to, you can still have many versions that define your particular type of Ascension. In any other topic, you may think it all a ruse from the complexities and versions describing this one word. Major religions all over the world demonstrate that people must have the ultimate chalice with everlasting life within to believe in. A seat at God's table is a definite bonus.

In the Biblical version, Christ dies, is resurrected back to life, then ascends into Heaven. This version of ascension is ascending into Heaven without necessarily dying first. But, even in this, there are several different versions.

Most major religions also have their versions of iconic people taken up or ascending to Heaven, or to be with God.

The following is a list of religions that have clearly defined representations of Ascension:
- Christianity and Catholicism
- Hellenism
- Hinduism
- Islam
- Judaism
- Zoroastrianism

Ascension as Spiritual Enlightenment

While a person is alive, Spiritual Enlightenment Ascension mostly is based on an event of complete comprehension of the person and everything in their perceptible universe coming into focus in a moment, accompanied by an overwhelming feeling of love, joy, and wholeness - living in the light.

"The ascension is a spiritual acceleration of consciousness that occurs after the natural conclusion of one's final lifetime on earth. It represents the point in the soul's evolution when it attains immortality. Through the ascension, the soul merges with the I AM Presence and returns to the Father-Mother God, free from the rounds of karma and reincarnation.
This process of returning to the source is recognized throughout the world's major religions, although the terminology used to describe it may differ." - Elizabeth Clare Prophet

Ascension and Transformation

Transformation - How you leave this world is not how you began

You have the ability to make substantial changes to yourself and your Karma in this plane of existence. It is an undertaking by your effort to make these changes. It will reshape your ideals and beliefs. Your personal energy will change likewise, and the people you attract into your circle will be different from those you attracted prior to your transformation. Therefore transformation is the product, the results of your actions, and the changes you have made. It should be an ongoing flux, as change is a keystone of living life.

Global / Mass Ascension - The Past is the Antithesis

To hold onto the past is to deconstruct Global or Mass Ascension. It is said that ascension causes a rewrite of the complete history of the planet. Why would this need to happen? Your history, your past, acts as an anchor. If people are meant to move forward to a new level of consciousness, then they cannot be anchored to the previous past [2]. (I am assigning numbers to make it easier for you to follow which "past" is being talked about. [1] would be the "new" past.)

As a new past [1] will be written, the old past [2] must be left behind and forgotten. As long as enough of the previous past [2] is let go to fulfil the requirements that change the global consciousness, then there may still be remnants; similar to the inconsistent remnants of ancient pasts [3, 4, 5,...] we see today. I am referring to the previous past [3] we left behind when the last change in consciousness happened. (Yes, it may be a bit confusing - like two steps forward then looking back one step to see what was there.)

The anchor is the global consciousness, as it has been constantly built over time creating and recreating our beliefs as - how things are meant to be. The global consciousness also acts as a self-fulfilling prophecy as to how we are to view and interpret the history of the planet: "It is ... Therefore, it is." It is only when you see outside the square and open your mind you begin to see the cracks. The cracks are there, and they are often massive. You just need to look for them.

The past [2] must be rewritten to create the new foundation of which the mass ascension process leads to. In this process, we would forget our previous past [2] as it is replaced by the new past [1]. There will likely be some inconsistencies. There are plenty of examples of the inconsistencies happening today that are most likely rollover from the last global "jump".

Previous Pasts [2, 3, 4...] Cause Inconsistencies; Cast Doubt on the Present

There have been discoveries out of the normal archaeological sequence that are dispelled as hoaxes or simply ignored. There are discoveries of the existence of life forms that are similar, but different to the accepted hominids, such as the giant races, which are documented in religious texts. Numerous reports over the last ~200 years, claim when the burial sites are discovered, it typically causes government cover-ups, seizure of the excavation, property, equipment, and evidence.

You may wonder why such discoveries would not be considered in the best interest for public disclosure. The answer is simple. Such discoveries would threaten the stability of the governments that are in power. Further to the outright lies, the governments in charge have the "one dominant species" theme to uphold. Anything that threatens that illusion is considered unacceptable. This may be the reason governments do not openly acknowledge that alien life forms - exist on Earth.

In every circumstance, governments claim their right to rule the people. If there was common knowledge of other races coexisting on the planet, even if they were not considered a superior race, their existence would trigger people to question the governments' right to rule; or which race is the ruling class?

Curiosity Kills a Cat?

Another anomaly that is not overly explored due to its' sensitivity has to do with aboriginal cultures that exist around the world. Their ability to carry the stories of what the tribe experienced in the past is amazing, as is their accuracy over time. Some aboriginals lay claim to histories of 40,000 years or more. That is quite extensive. How are the stories passed along? Through traditional forms of memory and song; a rhythm. Another means of assuring the oldest histories are projected forward is often in the form of petroglyphs, or rock carvings. To those that know how to read them, it is like reading the pages of a book. The sites where petroglyphs are found are often off limits to outsiders, as these are protected sacred sites.

There are some types of information the aboriginals do not like to reveal to outsiders. Sometimes outlandish methods are used to protect these characteristics or certain forms of knowledge. Out of respect for their desire to keep these details hidden; details that have been passed along to me from tribal elders, I cannot reveal them, unless I am released from my promise to keep the information sacred and secret. That is not likely to happen.

When Old School Meets New School Bureaucracy

One of the first attempts to formalise the recognition of Archaeology outside of the formally accepted timelines was the book "Forbidden Archaeology" (1993), which was subsequently banned from University campuses for challenging the way in which Archaeology is applied and taught. Some of the documentation may be controversial as to its origins, The work in its' entirety should not be summarily dismissed; as it is an ample weapon against stagnant, dogmatic teaching methods which should be open to change and other perspectives. Most universities do not like to be challenged, even though their entire existence is said to be based on learning; implying a stage for debate if details are to be challenged or updated.

Implementation of Confusing Benchmarks Set Stage - Mandela Effect

Previously, I mentioned that governments rely on people having a poor memory of events...

There have been a number of noticeable events, facts, and symbols that have been modified and changed over time. Only those people that have a very good memory tend to remember what the event or symbol really was before it was changed. Most people will likely say to themselves, "I must have not seen it right in the first place." Thus, they will dismiss the insertion of aberrations into their periphery. This is also referred to as the "Mandela Effect".

[You can read more about it by searching the Internet. You will usually feel it, like attempting to drive your car in the forward direction, just to find you are geared in reverse, resulting in a sudden, "What just happened?". A couple of classic examples are 'when and where' did **Nelson Mandela** die, and the symbolisms that have been added / changed in the *"The Wizard of Oz"* movie.]

Psychologically, this causes a "hole" in your clear understanding of the specifics or facts surrounding an event. Holes make you susceptible to hypnosis when you are unaware you are being hypnotised. Therefore, if the same hole can be placed in the majority of the population, the masses can be hypnotised into an action all at the same time. This is referred to as "mob psychology".

NOTE: Every year, the iconic movie, *"The Wizard of Oz"*, from 1939, is on TV. Certain symbolisms have been altered to change how the audience reacts to the content in the movie; as it is a subtle type of programming.

There can be a second reason why this is taking place. If those same key symbols are replaced by modified symbols, that represents something different to the population, it could be an attempt to influence the direction the global ascension to move in a different direction other than the direction it is meant to take. Earth is very unique in the Universe. If a change of global consciousness would happen in a way that is not the intended, correct way, then this Earth could be lost forever.

Ascension is the ultimate representation of thought power. As mentioned earlier, quantum physics explains that we and everything that "IS", are a mental construct of our thoughts giving birth to this holograph we reside within - our consciousness. If our thoughts (on a global basis) somehow become derailed, it could be catastrophic.

> *"Every living being is an engine geared to the wheelwork of the universe. Though seemingly affected only by its immediate surrounding, the sphere of external influence extends to infinite distance."*
> — Nikola Tesla

Personal Ascension - Giant Step in Your Spiritual Enlightenment

Within your personal consciousness, once you are one with the Universe and nothing material matters, and perhaps you have cleared your Karma where only positive remains, you may be able to shift your thought power to be ascended into Spiritual Enlightenment. Personal ascension is passing from living through your own ascension without dying first. You would be alive as you pass over into your newly formed consciousness. We are all nothing but energy. Some people that ascend decide to come back to this plane in the service of others, and assist them with their spiritual growth. Some of the names given to them would be Ascended Masters, Spirit Guides, or Angels.

NOTES

Chapter 9
Regarding Hope

Where there is hope...

OBSERVATIONS: You may have observed that even though I have written about a point in time - the tipping point of resources verses the population of Earth, I have additionally been writing about the future past that moment in our perceived time. That may seem to be inconsistent with the information presented here. However, the main topic here is "Consciousness", and not inconsistencies of time indexing.

There is hope.

Science has enabled us to live longer, healthier, and happier lives. But that may all be in vain. Anti-aging is no longer the gold chalice when everything around you collapses.

There is hope.

Yes, there may come a time when no amount of gold or silver will save you or any of us. There may come a time when horrendous acts are perpetrated by humans against each other, the likes of which have never been seen before. If there is one species on Earth that is capable of such vile acts, it is proven that only the human race is capable of such.

There is hope.

Our "big brain" got us into this mess. Only by using this big brain again will we ever hope to extricate ourselves from a dire fate. Preparations for dealing with the inevitable times ahead should have been underway about 50 years ago. Even 30 years ago may not be enough for preparations.

There is hope.

As the population of the Earth continues to spiral out of control, it becomes obvious there seems to be no clear plan of action in place. Is there a subversive plan in place; something unseen or hidden? Perhaps the movies and TV programs about global calamities and police shows with exceptional brutality are meant to prepare and desensitise you for a world that global authorities are predicting to unfold.

There is hope.

While everyone should encourage brain building for the masses, the global influences continue to degrade how and what the public is allowed to learn; and providing downward pressure against free thinking and innovative thought. The miasma of indecision the average person experiences each day is created from this delusional way of educating the masses. They are pawns; tranquilised to the big picture that looms before the world. The Great Unwashed. Sheeple.

There is hope.

In hope, I pray the deities of the cosmic consciousness and the quantum universe to find a suitable answer before the inevitable comes to pass - to rewrite our way through time and space to avoid such calamity.

There is always hope!

"The scientific man does not aim at an immediate result. He does not expect that his advanced ideas will be readily taken up. His work is like that of the planter — for the future. His duty is to lay the foundation for those who are to come, and point the way. He lives and labors and hopes."
— *Nikola Tesla*

Appendices

References

Pyramid Energy: The Philosophy of God, the Science of Man
by Dean Hardy (Author), Mary Hardy (Author), Marjorie Killick (Author) 1984

Forbidden Archaeology: The Hidden History of the Human Race
book by Michael A. Cremo and Richard L. Thompson 1993

Reports and Evidence of Giants Resource
http://www.sydhav.no/giants/newspapers.htm

1 in 6 Americans are on Psychiatric Drugs
https://www.livescience.com/57170-americans-psychiatrics-drug-use.html

HSAM (Highly Superior Autobiographical Memory) References...

McGaugh, J.L. Making lasting memories: Remembering the significant. Proceedings, National Academy of Sciences, USA, 110 (2), 2013, 10401-10407.

McGaugh, J.L. and Leport, A. Highly superior autobiographical memory. Scientific American, February 2014, 40-45.

Photo credits: MindtoMind.com, NASA, Wikipedia, Pixabay.com, FreeImages.com, clipart from Projideas.com

Hundredth Monkey Effect:

1. b c d Amundson, Ron (Summer 1985). Kendrick Frazier, ed. "The Hundredth Monkey Phenomenon". Skeptical Inquirer: 348–356.
2. Blair, Lawrence (1975). Rhythms of Vision: The Changing Patterns of Belief. London: Croom Helm Ltd. ISBN 978-0-8052-3610-1.
3. Blair, unlike Watson, does not assign the date 1952 to the observations.
4. Keys, Ken (1984). The Hundredth Monkey. Camarillo: DeVorss & Co. ISBN 0-942024-01-X.
5. Whiten, Andrew; J. Goodall; W. C. McGrew; T. Nishida; V. Reynolds; Y. Sugiyama; C. E. G. Tutin; R. W. Wrangham; C. Boesch (1999). "Cultures in chimpanzees". Nature. 399 (6737): 682–685. doi:10.1038/21415. PMID 10385119.
6. Boesch, Christophe (2012). "31. Culture in primates. A - Culture as it Happens". In Jaan Valsiner. The Oxford Handbook of Culture and Psychology (PDF). OUP. p. 678. ISBN 9780195396430.
7. Trivedi, Bijal P. (February 6, 2004). ""Hot Tub Monkeys" Offer Eye on Nonhuman "Culture"". National Geographic Channel October 28, 2010/National Geographic.
8. b Galef, B. G. (1992). "The question of animal culture". Human Nature. 3 (2): 157–178. doi:10.1007/BF02692251.
9. Wikipedia.org

Article 1

New Vision With Weather – When It Rains, It Pours

"When I Wash My Car, it Rains"

Storm Clouds

Imagine if something as simple as washing your car could change the weather. WOW! What a world it would be.

I recently asked someone, *"Have you ever washed your car, and as soon as you are done, it begins to rain?"* He immediately answered, *"Yes, it happens to me all the time."* Many people just know it will rain if they wash their car.

A Road Less Travelled

Let's take a walk down a road less travelled, and explore the possibilities of that one statement, *"Whenever I wash my car, it rains."* It is a true statement to most people. (Of course you must have a car to wash in the first place.) Could people benefit globally thinking about things this way? *"There wasn't a cloud in the sky when I started, but by the time I finished washing my car, the thunderheads were upon us."* What if weather could be influenced that way?

Weather in the Public Eye

What is the single major topic that is in the minds of most people, most days of their life? It is suggested if you want to start a conversation, talk about the weather. Everyone has an opinion. Yes, weather is the main topic of interest.

Other issues will come and go. There are only so many stories about famous people, governments, or any number of transient events that draw your attention. But there are none that match the day to day resiliency as the weather. In recent times, weather has been even bigger in the news than ever before. Topics of interests such as global warming, climate change, El Niño, polar ice caps melting, ice age, and the excessive list goes on.

Now that the experts have pummelled us with enough information to make us all climate change savvy, many of their scientific findings and claims have been repudiated for inaccuracy. Gaia, Mother Nature, has easily defeated their flamboyant efforts with a blast from volcanoes spewing out massive amounts of greenhouse gases into the air. It makes human contribution to greenhouse gases insignificant in comparison.

New Vision with Weather

What if there was a completely different way to deal with weather, as well as other things? What if the human spirit could be harnessed to deal with these issues energetically? Guess what? It has already been underway for thousands of years. I am not reporting on some new-fangled idea.

I am about to take you on a fantastic journey of understanding the simple complexities of the human mind, and how it can be used in global consciousness to change the outcome of events. THIS IS NOT NEW! The same practice has been done for thousands of years by various religious and spiritual organizations to influence the direction of our planet by moving the minds and hearts of man in directions benefiting man-kind.

For Spiritual Reference

Common examples in use are specific prayers or mantras that seek to communicate the higher good to the minds of others. When a group of people create a singular thought, it strengthens the output. The larger the group, the more power is behind sending out the directed energetic message. Again, most of these types of spiritual or religious undertaking deal with the highest good when it comes to global consciousness. What are the characteristics of a spiritual person?

What if we were to use this same principal idea coupled with the Law of Attraction to influence weather patterns? Traditional cultures around the world recognize the "Shaman", "Weather Witch" or "Rain Man". This is usually a person that has a spiritual connection with the elements such as spiritual meaning of your name. This person acts as a liaison between the people in need and the forces of nature. Secondly, they coordinate the group of people, or tribe, to be in like-minded unison to draw in the elements needed; in this case, rain.

Drought is obviously caused by the lack of rain. So, quite often in the work to break the drought and make it rain, there may be a rain dance where everyone is dancing in a rhythmic pattern to resemble or entice rain to come. This is not a social gathering. This is considered a serious enument of body, mind, and soul. For many people their survival is at stake. During the dancing, which may go on for many hours, heightened states of consciousness are often reached, and contact with spirit guides may be sought.

Other people that work with vibrational energy to influence the elements include geomancers, dowsers, witch doctors, shamen, and Tribal Elders.

Taxing Rain

Now, let's take this scenario one step further. Let's paint a picture. As more and more governments are grabbing money from wherever they can, let's look at how the balance could be tipped by a government charging for or taxing rain. You are probably thinking, *"That's ludicrous! That is impossible! How could a government ever justify charging someone for rain?"* Yes, it is already happening. Here is how.

A farmer digs a dam on his property to catch water when it falls from the sky, so he can water his crops and does not need to rely on regular rain. The farmer then sets out to provide the pumps, power (usually some form of electricity), valves, piping, and the entire infrastructure to move the water from his dam to where it is needed. This is a great investment for the farmer and costs him out of pocket before he can grow his crops to pay back the money for the dam. It may take years of growth to pay for that investment.

Along comes an official that assesses the dam and declares that since the farmer will be using the water to create crops that <u>may</u> produce an income, that he will be taxed by the volume of water the dam can hold, whether it currently has a drop of water in it or not. Then along comes the water department and installs a gauge onto the output piping the farmer paid for, to further monitor his use of the water that has fallen from the sky. Therefore the farmer has created a huge bill for himself, and the government is now taxing him for his effort to create something out of nothing.

Lessons in the Law of Attraction

Do you think the farmer may feel some resentment? Maybe he would feel that he is already paying his way with regards to the government. So, for every bit of water he uses from his own dam, he will now be charged; even though the government did not give him a penny to compensate his effort. *They didn't even pick up a shovel.*

This next part may sound like self-sabotage, and it is. Since the farmer doesn't like what has just been pulled on him, he may inadvertently look at his dam, and even the rain to fill it, as a burden he cannot afford. How is he supposed to catch the rain, water and grow his crops, sell them, and do all that work, just to have the government there with bill in hand collecting the rain money from him without them putting any effort in to help him run his farm? This could be setting up such a vibration around his farm that it may not rain for years.

So if you ever hear that it is impossible for you to pay for the rain you receive, or even the air you breathe, think again. It is just a matter of time before it affects you directly. You are probably paying for it already at the checkout counter of the grocery store.

Epilogue: Direct Mass Consciousness for Weather Control
It is time to put a *positive spin* on washing your car during a drought. In times of drought, the government can mandate (That seems to be what governments like doing.) that everyone wash their car on a specific day each month. Therefore, most people will be washing their

car on the same day. Just think how many people would be automatically thinking, *"Every time I wash my car, it rains."* With that amount of concentrated mental energy shouting out that it is going to rain, the clouds will be driven to appear and provide.

You may think I have gone too far with this. That is fine. You have your spiritual opinion. Whenever you carry vast amounts of accessible information, you can flow between the logical, psychological, and the esoteric world at will. The information you don't have available are the personal results my clients tell me about when they employ it for themselves… Amazing!

Believe that you can move mountains, and you will.

Great Things Happen Here!

This article can be found at http://mindtomind.com/weather-when-it-rains-it-pours/

Appendix I

Continuation of United Nations Report...

PARIS, 6 May – Nature is declining globally at rates unprecedented in human history – and the rate of species extinctions is accelerating, with grave impacts on people around the world now likely, warns a landmark new report from the Intergovernmental Science-Policy Platform on Biodiversity and Ecosystem Services (IPBES), the summary of which was approved at the 7th session of the IPBES Plenary, meeting last week (29 April – 4 May) in Paris.

"The overwhelming evidence of the IPBES Global Assessment, from a wide range of different fields of knowledge, presents an ominous picture," said IPBES Chair, Sir Robert Watson. "The health of ecosystems on which we and all other species depend is deteriorating more rapidly than ever. We are eroding the very foundations of our economies, livelihoods, food security, health and quality of life worldwide."

"The Report also tells us that it is not too late to make a difference, but only if we start now at every level from local to global," he said. "Through 'transformative change', nature can still be conserved, restored and used sustainably – this is also key to meeting most other global goals. By transformative change, we mean a fundamental, system-wide reorganization across technological, economic and social factors, including paradigms, goals and values."

"The member States of IPBES Plenary have now acknowledged that, by its very nature, transformative change can expect opposition from those with interests vested in the status quo, but also that such opposition can be overcome for the broader public good," Watson said.

The IPBES Global Assessment Report on Biodiversity and Ecosystem Services is the most comprehensive ever completed. It is the first intergovernmental Report of its kind and builds on the landmark Millennium Ecosystem Assessment of 2005, introducing innovative ways of evaluating evidence.

Compiled by 145 expert authors from 50 countries over the past three years, with inputs from another 310 contributing authors, the Report assesses changes over the past five decades, providing a comprehensive picture of the relationship between economic development pathways and their impacts on nature. It also offers a range of possible scenarios for the coming decades.

Based on the systematic review of about 15,000 scientific and government sources, the Report also draws (for the first time ever at this scale) on indigenous and local knowledge, particularly addressing issues relevant to Indigenous Peoples and Local Communities.

"Biodiversity and nature's contributions to people are our common heritage and humanity's most important life-supporting 'safety net'. But our safety net is stretched almost to breaking point," said Prof. Sandra Díaz (Argentina), who co-chaired the Assessment with Prof. Josef Settele (Germany) and Prof. Eduardo S. Brondízio (Brazil and USA).

"The diversity within species, between species and of ecosystems, as well as many fundamental contributions we derive from nature, are declining fast, although we still have the means to ensure a sustainable future for people and the planet."

The Report finds that around 1 million animal and plant species are now threatened with extinction, many within decades, more than ever before in human history.

The average abundance of native species in most major land-based habitats has fallen by at least 20%, mostly since 1900. More than 40% of amphibian species, almost 33% of reef-forming corals and more than a third of all marine mammals are threatened. The picture is less clear for insect species, but available evidence supports a tentative estimate of 10% being threatened. At least 680 vertebrate species had been driven to extinction since the 16th century and more than 9% of all domesticated breeds of mammals used for food and agriculture had become extinct by 2016, with at least 1,000 more breeds still threatened.

"Ecosystems, species, wild populations, local varieties and breeds of domesticated plants and animals are shrinking, deteriorating or vanishing. The essential, interconnected web of life on Earth is getting smaller and increasingly frayed," said Prof. Settele. "This loss is a direct result of human activity and constitutes a direct threat to human well-being in all regions of the world."

To increase the policy-relevance of the Report, the assessment's authors have ranked, for the first time at this scale and based on a thorough analysis of the available evidence, the five direct drivers of change in nature with the largest relative global impacts so far. These culprits are, in descending order: (1) changes in land and sea use; (2) direct exploitation of organisms; (3) climate change; (4) pollution and (5) invasive alien species.

The Report notes that, since 1980, greenhouse gas emissions have doubled, raising average global temperatures by at least 0.7 degrees Celsius – with climate change already impacting nature from the level of ecosystems to that of genetics – impacts expected to increase over the coming decades, in some cases surpassing the impact of land and sea use change and other drivers.

Despite progress to conserve nature and implement policies, the Report also finds that global goals for conserving and sustainably using nature and achieving sustainability cannot be met by current trajectories, and goals for 2030 and beyond may only be achieved through transformative changes across economic, social, political and technological factors. With good progress on components of only four of the 20 Aichi Biodiversity Targets, it is likely that most will be missed by the 2020 deadline. Current negative trends in biodiversity and ecosystems will undermine progress towards 80% (35 out of 44) of the assessed targets of the Sustainable Development Goals, related to poverty, hunger, health, water, cities, climate, oceans and land (SDGs 1, 2, 3, 6, 11, 13, 14 and 15). Loss of biodiversity is therefore shown to be not only an environmental issue, but also a developmental, economic, security, social and moral issue as well.

"To better understand and, more importantly, to address the main causes of damage to biodiversity and nature's contributions to people, we need to understand the history and global interconnection of complex demographic and economic indirect drivers of change, as well as the social values that underpin them," said Prof. Brondízio. "Key indirect drivers include increased population and per capita consumption; technological innovation, which in some cases has lowered and in other cases increased the damage to nature; and, critically, issues of governance and accountability. A pattern that emerges is one of global interconnectivity and 'telecoupling' – with resource extraction and production often occurring in one part of the world to satisfy the needs of distant consumers in other regions."

Other notable findings of the Report include:

Three-quarters of the land-based environment and about 66% of the marine environment have been significantly altered by human actions. On average these trends have been less severe or avoided in areas held or managed by Indigenous Peoples and Local Communities.

More than a third of the world's land surface and nearly 75% of freshwater resources are now devoted to crop or livestock production.

The value of agricultural crop production has increased by about 300% since 1970, raw timber harvest has risen by 45% and approximately 60 billion tons of renewable and nonrenewable resources are now extracted globally every year – having nearly doubled since 1980.

Land degradation has reduced the productivity of 23% of the global land surface, up to US$577 billion in annual global crops are at risk from pollinator loss and 100-300 million people are at increased risk of floods and hurricanes because of loss of coastal habitats and protection.

In 2015, 33% of marine fish stocks were being harvested at unsustainable levels; 60% were maximally sustainably fished, with just 7% harvested at levels lower than what can be sustainably fished.

Urban areas have more than doubled since 1992.

Plastic pollution has increased tenfold since 1980, 300-400 million tons of heavy metals, solvents, toxic sludge and other wastes from industrial facilities are dumped annually into the world's waters, and fertilizers entering coastal ecosystems have produced more than 400 ocean 'dead zones', totalling more than 245,000 km2 (591-595) – a combined area greater than that of the United Kingdom.

Negative trends in nature will continue to 2050 and beyond in all of the policy scenarios explored in the Report, except those that include transformative change – due to the projected impacts of increasing land-use change, exploitation of organisms and climate change, although with significant differences between regions.

The Report also presents a wide range of illustrative actions for sustainability and pathways for achieving them across and between sectors such as agriculture, forestry, marine systems, freshwater systems, urban areas, energy, finance and many others. It highlights the importance of, among others, adopting integrated management and cross-sectoral approaches that take into account the trade-offs of food and energy production, infrastructure, freshwater and coastal management, and biodiversity conservation.

Also identified as a key element of more sustainable future policies is the evolution of global financial and economic systems to build a global sustainable economy, steering away from the current limited paradigm of economic growth.

"IPBES presents the authoritative science, knowledge and the policy options to decision-makers for their consideration," said IPBES Executive Secretary, Dr. Anne Larigauderie. "We thank the hundreds of experts, from around the world, who have volunteered their time and knowledge to help address the loss of species, ecosystems and genetic diversity – a truly global and generational threat to human well-being."

Further Information on Key Issues from the Report

Scale of Loss of Nature

Gains from societal and policy responses, while important, have not stopped massive losses. Since 1970, trends in agricultural production, fish harvest, bioenergy production and harvest of materials have increased, in response to population growth, rising demand and technological development, this has come at a steep price, which has been unequally distributed within and across countries. Many other key indicators of nature's contributions to people however, such as soil organic carbon and pollinator diversity, have declined, indicating that gains in material contributions are often not sustainable .

The pace of agricultural expansion into intact ecosystems has varied from country to country. Losses of intact ecosystems have occurred primarily in the tropics, home to the highest levels of biodiversity on the planet. For example, 100 million hectares of tropical forest were lost from 1980 to 2000, resulting mainly from cattle ranching in Latin America (about 42 million hectares) and plantations in South-East Asia (about 7.5 million hectares, of which 80% is for palm oil, used mostly in food, cosmetics, cleaning products and fuel) among others.

Since 1970 the global human population has more than doubled (from 3.7 to 7.6 billion), rising unevenly across countries and regions; and per capita gross domestic product is four times higher – with ever-more distant consumers shifting the environmental burden of consumption and production across regions.

The average abundance of native species in most major land-based habitats has fallen by at least 20%, mostly since 1900.

The numbers of invasive alien species per country have risen by about 70% since 1970, across the 21 countries with detailed records.

The distributions of almost half (47%) of land-based flightless mammals, for example, and almost a quarter of threatened birds, may already have been negatively affected by climate change.

Indigenous Peoples, Local Communities and Nature

At least a quarter of the global land area is traditionally owned, managed, used or occupied by Indigenous Peoples. These areas include approximately 35% of the area that is formally protected, and approximately 35% of all remaining terrestrial areas with very low human intervention.

Nature managed by Indigenous Peoples and Local Communities is under increasing pressure but is generally declining less rapidly than in other lands – although 72% of local indicators developed and used by Indigenous Peoples and Local Communities show the deterioration of nature that underpins local livelihoods.

The areas of the world projected to experience significant negative effects from global changes in climate, biodiversity, ecosystem functions and nature's contributions to people are also areas in which large concentrations of Indigenous Peoples and many of the world's poorest communities reside.

Regional and global scenarios currently lack and would benefit from an explicit consideration of the views, perspectives and rights of Indigenous Peoples and Local Communities, their knowledge and understanding of large regions and ecosystems, and their desired future development pathways. Recognition of the knowledge, innovations and practices, institutions and values of Indigenous Peoples and Local Communities and their inclusion and participation in environmental governance often enhances their quality of life, as well as nature conservation, restoration and sustainable use. Their positive contributions to sustainability can be facilitated through national recognition of land tenure, access and resource rights in accordance with national legislation, the application of free, prior and informed consent, and improved collaboration, fair and equitable sharing of benefits arising from the use, and co-management arrangements with local communities.

Global Targets and Policy Scenarios

Past and ongoing rapid declines in biodiversity, ecosystem functions and many of nature's contributions to people mean that most international societal and environmental goals, such as those embodied in the Aichi Biodiversity Targets and the 2030 Agenda for Sustainable Development will not be achieved based on current trajectories.

The authors of the Report examined six policy scenarios – very different 'baskets' of clustered policy options and approaches, including 'Regional Competition', 'Business as Usual' and 'Global Sustainability' – projecting the likely impacts on biodiversity and nature's contributions to people of these pathways by 2050. They concluded that, except in scenarios that include transformative change, the negative trends in nature, ecosystem functions and in many of nature's contributions to people will continue to 2050 and beyond due to the projected impacts of increasing land and sea use change, exploitation of organisms and climate change.

Policy Tools, Options and Exemplary Practices

Policy actions and societal initiatives are helping to raise awareness about the impact of consumption on nature, protecting local environments, promoting sustainable local economies and restoring degraded areas. Together with initiatives at various levels these have contributed to expanding and strengthening the current network of ecologically representative and well-connected protected area networks and other effective area-based conservation measures, the protection of watersheds and incentives and sanctions to reduce pollution .

The Report presents an illustrative list of possible actions and pathways for achieving them across locations, systems and scales, which will be most likely to support sustainability. Taking an integrated approach:

In *agriculture*, the Report emphasizes, among others: promoting good agricultural and agroecological practices; multifunctional landscape planning (which simultaneously provides food security, livelihood opportunities, maintenance of species and ecological functions) and cross-sectoral integrated management. It also points to the importance of deeper engagement of all actors throughout the food system (including producers, the public sector, civil society and consumers) and more integrated landscape and watershed management; conservation of the diversity of genes, varieties, cultivars, breeds, landraces and species; as well as approaches that empower consumers and producers through market transparency, improved distribution and localization (that revitalizes local economies), reformed supply chains and reduced food waste.

In *marine systems*, the Report highlights, among others: ecosystem-based approaches to fisheries management; spatial planning; effective quotas; marine protected areas; protecting and managing key marine biodiversity areas; reducing run- off pollution into oceans and working closely with producers and consumers.

In *freshwater systems*, policy options and actions include, among others: more inclusive water governance for collaborative water management and greater equity; better integration of water resource management and landscape planning across scales; promoting practices to reduce soil erosion, sedimentation and pollution run-off; increasing water storage; promoting investment in water projects with clear sustainability criteria; as well as addressing the fragmentation of many freshwater policies.

In *urban areas*, the Report highlights, among others: promotion of nature-based solutions; increasing access to urban services and a healthy urban environment for low-income communities; improving access to green spaces; sustainable production and consumption and ecological connectivity within urban spaces, particularly with native species.

Across all examples, the Report recognises the importance of including different value systems and diverse interests and worldviews in formulating policies and actions. This includes the full and effective participation of Indigenous Peoples and Local Communities in governance, the reform and development of incentive structures and ensuring that biodiversity considerations are prioritised across all key sector planning.

"We have already seen the first stirrings of actions and initiatives for transformative change, such as innovative policies by many countries, local authorities and businesses, but especially by young people worldwide," said Sir Robert Watson. "From the young global shapers behind the #VoiceforthePlanet movement, to school strikes for climate, there is a groundswell of understanding that urgent action is needed if we are to secure anything approaching a sustainable future. The IPBES Global Assessment Report offers the best available expert evidence to help inform these decisions, policies and actions – and provides the scientific basis for the biodiversity framework and new decadal targets for biodiversity, to be decided in late 2020 in China, under the auspices of the UN Convention on Biological Diversity."

By the Numbers – Key Statistics and Facts from the Report

General

75%: terrestrial environment "severely altered" to date by human actions (marine environments 66%)

47%: reduction in global indicators of ecosystem extent and condition against their estimated natural baselines, with many continuing to decline by at least 4% per decade

28%: global land area held and/or managed by Indigenous Peoples , including >40% of formally protected areas and 37% of all remaining terrestrial areas with very low human intervention

+/-60 billion: tons of renewable and non-renewable resources extracted globally each year, up nearly 100% since 1980

15%: increase in global per capita consumption of materials since 1980

>85%: of wetlands present in 1700 had been lost by 2000 – loss of wetlands is currently three times faster, in percentage terms, than forest loss.

Species, Populations and Varieties of Plants and Animals

8 million: total estimated number of animal and plant species on Earth (including 5.5 million insect species)

Tens to hundreds of times: the extent to which the current rate of global species extinction is higher compared to average over the last 10 million years, and the rate is accelerating

Up to 1 million: species threatened with extinction, many within decades

>500,000 (+/-9%): share of the world's estimated 5.9 million terrestrial species with insufficient habitat for long term survival without habitat restoration

>40%: amphibian species threatened with extinction

Almost 33%: reef forming corals, sharks and shark relatives, and >33% marine mammals threatened with extinction

25%: average proportion of species threatened with extinction across terrestrial, freshwater and marine vertebrate, invertebrate and plant groups that have been studied in sufficient detail

At least 680: vertebrate species driven to extinction by human actions since the 16th century

+/-10%: tentative estimate of proportion of insect species threatened with extinction

>20%: decline in average abundance of native species in most major terrestrial biomes, mostly since 1900

+/-560 (+/-10%): domesticated breeds of mammals were extinct by 2016, with at least 1,000 more threatened

3.5%: domesticated breed of birds extinct by 2016

70%: increase since 1970 in numbers of invasive alien species across 21 countries with detailed records

30%: reduction in global terrestrial habitat integrity caused by habitat loss and deterioration

47%: proportion of terrestrial flightless mammals and 23% of threatened birds whose distributions may have been negatively impacted by climate change already

>6: species of ungulate (hoofed mammals) would likely be extinct or surviving only in captivity today without conservation measures

Food and Agriculture

300%: increase in food crop production since 1970

23%: land areas that have seen a reduction in productivity due to land degradation

>75%: global food crop types that rely on animal pollination

US$235 to US$577 billion: annual value of global crop output at risk due to pollinator loss

5.6 gigatons: annual CO_2 emissions sequestered in marine and terrestrial ecosystems – equivalent to 60% of global fossil fuel emission

+/-11%: world population that is undernourished

100 million: hectares of agricultural expansion in the tropics from 1980 to 2000, mainly cattle ranching in Latin America (+/-42 million ha), and plantations in Southeast Asia (+/-7.5 million ha, of which 80% is oil palm), half of it at the expense of intact forests

3%: increase in land transformation to agriculture between 1992 and 2015, mostly at the expense of forests

>33%: world's land surface (and +/-75% of freshwater resources) devoted to crop or livestock production

12%: world's ice-free land used for crop production

25%: world's ice-free land used for grazing (+/-70% of drylands)

+/-25%: greenhouse gas emissions caused by land clearing, crop production and fertilization, with animal-based food contributing 75% to that figure

+/-30%: global crop production and global food supply provided by small land holdings (<2 ha), using +/-25% of agricultural land, usually maintaining rich agrobiodiversity

$100 billion: estimated level of financial support in OECD countries (2015) to agriculture that is potentially harmful to the environment

Oceans and Fishing

33%: marine fish stocks in 2015 being harvested at unsustainable levels; 60% are maximally sustainably fished; 7% are underfished

>55%: ocean area covered by industrial fishing

3-10%: projected decrease in ocean net primary production due to climate change alone by the end of the century

3-25%: projected decrease in fish biomass by the end of the century in low and high climate warming scenarios, respectively

>90%: proportion of the global commercial fishers accounted for by small scale fisheries (over 30 million people) – representing nearly 50% of global fish catch

Up to 33%: estimated share in 2011 of world's reported fish catch that is illegal, unreported or unregulated

>10%: decrease per decade in the extent of seagrass meadows from 1970-2000

+/-50%: live coral cover of reefs lost since 1870s

100-300 million: people in coastal areas at increased risk due to loss of coastal habitat protection

400: low oxygen (hypoxic) coastal ecosystem 'dead zones' caused by fertilizers, affecting >245,000 km2

29%: average reduction in the extinction risk for mammals and birds in 109 countries thanks to conservation investments from 1996 to 2008; the extinction risk of birds, mammals and amphibians would have been at least 20% greater without conservation action in recent decade

>107: highly threatened birds, mammals and reptiles estimated to have benefitted from the eradication of invasive mammals on islands

Forests

45%: increase in raw timber production since 1970 (4 billion cubic meters in 2017)

+/-13 million: forestry industry jobs

50%: agricultural expansion that occurred at the expense of forests

50%: decrease in net rate of forest loss since the 1990s (excluding those managed for timber or agricultural extraction)

68%: global forest area today compared with the estimated pre-industrial level

7%: reduction of intact forests (>500 sq. km with no human pressure) from 2000-2013 in developed and developing countries

290 million ha (+/-6%): native forest cover lost from 1990-2015 due to clearing and wood harvesting

110 million ha: rise in the area of planted forests from 1990-2015

10-15%: global timber supplies provided by illegal forestry (up to 50% in some areas)

>2 billion: people who rely on wood fuel to meet their primary energy needs

Mining and Energy

<1%: total land used for mining, but the industry has significant negative impacts on biodiversity, emissions, water quality and human health

+/-17,000: large-scale mining sites (in 171 countries), mostly managed by 616 international corporations

+/-6,500: offshore oil and gas ocean mining installations ((in 53 countries)

US$345 billion: global subsidies for fossil fuels resulting in US$5 trillion in overall costs, including nature deterioration externalities; coal accounts for 52% of post-tax subsidies, petroleum for +/-33% and natural gas for +/-10%

Urbanization, Development and Socioeconomic Issues

>100%: growth of urban areas since 1992

25 million km: length of new paved roads foreseen by 2050, with 90% of construction in least developed and developing countries

+/-50,000: number of large dams (>15m height) ; +/-17 million reservoirs (>0.01 ha)

105%: increase in global human population (from 3.7 to 7.6 billion) since 1970 unevenly across countries and regions

50 times higher: per capita GDP in developed vs. least developed countries

>2,500: conflicts over fossil fuels, water, food and land currently occurring worldwide

>1,000: environmental activists and journalists killed between 2002 and 2013

Health

70%: proportion of cancer drugs that are natural or synthetic products inspired by nature

+/-4 billion: people who rely primarily on natural medicines

17%: infectious diseases spread by animal vectors, causing >700,000 annual deaths

+/-821 million: people face food insecurity in Asia and Africa

40%: of the global population lacks access to clean and safe drinking water

>80%: global wastewater discharged untreated into the environment

300-400 million tons: heavy metals, solvents, toxic sludge, and other wastes from industrial facilities dumped annually into the world's waters

10 times: increase in plastic pollution since 1980

Climate Change

1 degree Celsius: average global temperature difference in 2017 compared to pre-industrial levels, rising +/-0.2 (+/-0.1) degrees Celsius per decade

>3 mm: annual average global sea level rise over the past two decades

16-21 cm: rise in global average sea level since 1900

100% increase since 1980 in greenhouse gas emissions, raising average global temperature by at least 0.7 degree

40%: rise in carbon footprint of tourism (to 4.5Gt of carbon dioxide) from 2009 to 2013

8%: of total greenhouse gas emissions are from transport and food consumption related to tourism

5%: estimated fraction of species at risk of extinction from 2°C warming alone, rising to 16% at 4.3°C warming

Even for global warming of 1.5 to 2 degrees, the majority of terrestrial species ranges are projected to shrink profoundly.

Sustainable Development Goals

Most: Aichi Biodiversity Targets for 2020 likely to be missed

22 of 44: assessed targets under the Sustainable Development Goals related to poverty, hunger, health, water, cities, climate, ocean and land are being undermined by substantial negative trends in nature and its contributions to people

72%: of local indicators in nature developed and used by Indigenous Peoples and Local Communities that show negative trends

4: number of Aichi Targets where good progress has been made on certain components, with moderate progress on some components of another 7 targets, poor progress on all components of 6 targets, and insufficient information to assess progress on some or all components of the remaining 3 targets

IPBES Partner Comments

"Nature makes human development possible but our relentless demand for the earth's resources is accelerating extinction rates and devastating the world's ecosystems. UN Environment is proud to support the Global Assessment Report produced by the Intergovernmental Science-Policy Platform on Biodiversity and Ecosystem Services because it highlights the critical need to integrate biodiversity considerations in global decision-making on any sector or challenge, whether its water or agriculture, infrastructure or business."
– **Joyce Msuya**, Acting Head, UN Environment

"Across cultures, humans inherently value nature. The magic of seeing fireflies flickering long into the night is immense. We draw energy and nutrients from nature. We find sources of food, medicine, livelihoods and innovation in nature. Our well-being fundamentally depends on nature. Our efforts to conserve biodiversity and ecosystems must be underpinned by the best science that humanity can produce. This is why the scientific evidence compiled in this IPBES Global Assessment is so important. It will help us build a stronger foundation for shaping the post 2020 global biodiversity framework: the 'New Deal for Nature and People'; and for achieving the SDGs."
– **Achim Steiner**, Administrator, United Nations Development Programme

"This essential report reminds each of us of the obvious truth: the present generations have the responsibility to bequeath to future generations a planet that is not irreversibly damaged by human activity. Our local, indigenous and scientific knowledge are proving that we have solutions and so no more excuses: we must live on earth differently. UNESCO is committed to promoting respect of the living and of its diversity, ecological solidarity with other living species, and to establish new, equitable and global links of partnership and intragenerational solidarity, for the perpetuation of humankind."
– **Audrey Azoulay**, Director-General, UNESCO

"The IPBES' 2019 Global Assessment Report on Biodiversity and Ecosystem Services comes at a critical time for the planet and all its peoples. The report's findings – and the years of diligent work by the many scientists who contributed – will offer a comprehensive view of the current conditions of global biodiversity. Healthy biodiversity is the essential infrastructure that supports all forms of life on earth, including human life. It also provides nature-based solutions on many of the most critical environmental, economic, and social challenges that we face as human society, including climate change, sustainable development, health, and water and food security. We are currently in the midst of preparing for the 2020 UN Biodiversity Conference, in China, which will mark the close of the Aichi Biodiversity Targets and set the course for a post 2020 ecologically focused sustainable development pathway to deliver multiple benefits for people, the planet and our global economy. The IPBES report will serve

as a fundamental baseline of where we are and where we need to go as a global community to inspire humanity to reach the 2050 Vision of the UN Biodiversity Convention "Living in harmony with nature". I want to extend my thanks and congratulations to the IPBES community for their hard work, immense contributions and continued partnership."
– **Cristiana Pasca Palmer**, Executive Secretary, Convention on Biological Diversity

"The Global Assessment of biodiversity and ecosystem services adds a major element to the body of evidence for the importance of biodiversity to efforts to achieve the Zero Hunger objective and meet the Sustainable Development Goals. Together, assessments undertaken by IPBES, FAO, CBD and other organizations point to the urgent need for action to better conserve and sustainably use biodiversity and to the importance of cross-sectoral and multidisciplinary collaboration among decision-makers and other stakeholders at all levels."
– **Jose Graziano da Silva**, Director-General, Food and Agriculture Organization of the United Nations

Original document at United Nations Internet site:
https://www.un.org/sustainabledevelopment/blog/2019/05/nature-decline-unprecedented-report/)

Dr Shannon Panzo, photographic memory expert, brain management and mental photography mentor, brings thought-provoking topics into focus to intrigue mankind. Consciousness is hotly debated with each answer only leading to more questions. His enigmatic style supports infinite learning the universe has for each of us.

"Life is not meant to be orderly, more like a collection of random events we consider and learn by." - Dr. Shannon Panzo.

More fascinating books by Dr Shannon Panzo.

Are You Living Under the Jackfruit Tree?
(Great Things Happen Here! Book 1)   ASIN: B007W0U6X2

Great things happen here! It's true, and when you've read this book you'll understand why, and what the Jackfruit tree is. An introduction to concepts that will change your view of intelligence, of reading, to the very core of learning. If you think you know about speed reading, photographic memory, or eidetic memory, think again. Dr Shannon Panzo introduces the concept of "Mental Photography" and his "ZOX Pro Training" system which makes traditional 'speed reading' look very slow.

Revealing Truth Under The Jackfruit Tree
(Great Things Happen Here! Book 2)   ASIN: B00A9VC5JE

This book deals with realization and awakening, continues to explore the fascinating thoughts of author Shannon Panzo, imparting teachings, musings and thought-provoking nuggets in his eclectic style.

Chrysalis Transformation Under the Jackfruit Tree

(Great Things Happen Here! Book 3)   ASIN: B00AN055R0

The third book in the series takes you on a journey of awakening and mental progress. It is all about preparation for what will become the future you build for yourself. Climb into your mental chrysalis, and a metamorphosis transforms you; preparing for the emergence of your inner butterfly.

NOTES

www.ingramcontent.com/pod-product-compliance
Lightning Source LLC
Chambersburg PA
CBHW062100290426

44110CB00022B/2658